Boundaries Over Bullsh*t

5-Step Guide: Stop People-Pleasing,
Say No Without Guilt, and Trust Yourself Again

M. Luna Zidane

For R.T., L.S., S.M., N.D.M., A.P.C.M., K.J.Y., and M.R.R.

*Thank you for being such beautiful examples of loving givers
who are learning, slowly and courageously, to give back to yourselves.*

May your boundaries rise as boldly as your hearts love.

Table of Contents

Free Bonus Gift   VII

Author's Note   IX

Introduction   XI

1. You're Not Tired — You're Overextended   1

2. The Five-Step Boundary Blueprint   9

3. The Relationships That Know How to Get to You   17

4. You Are Not a Hotline — Reclaiming Your Attention   27

5. The Boundary Scripts Vault   33

6. When the Pushback Arrives — And It Will   47

7. When Your Body Panics at Boundaries   57

8. Holding Your Ground When Life Gets Loud   67

9. Who You Become When You Stop Shrinking   75

10. The Woman on the Other Side   83

11. Beyond Boundaries — The Life You're Building Now   89

Conclusion   97

Epilogue   101

A Note on Reviews   105

Further Reading   107

About the Author   115

Free Bonus Gift

As a thank-you for purchasing *Boundaries Over Bullsh*t*, you get free access to 9 worksheets designed to take everything you learned in this book and make it work in your actual life.

These worksheets will help you:

- Identify exactly where your energy is leaking — and what to do about it.

- Stop over-explaining, over-giving, and over-functioning in the relationships that drain you most.

- Build limits your body can actually trust, so boundary conversations stop feeling like emergencies.

- Translate the scripts and frameworks from this book into your specific situations.

- Track your progress so you can see how far you've come, even on the days it doesn't feel like it.

This isn't busywork. It's the practical side of the work you've already started — for the real-life moments when boundaries matter most and feel hardest to hold.

Scan the QR code below to claim your free access.

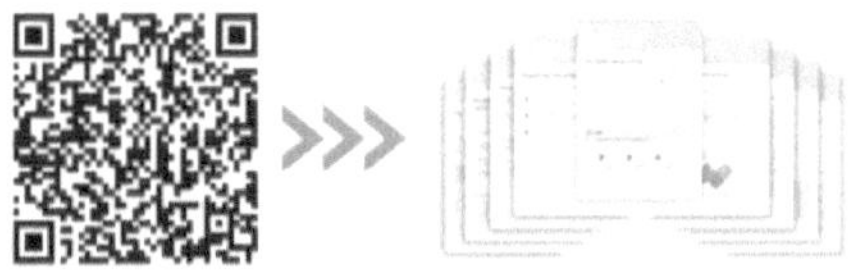

This is my way of continuing the work with you — because reading about boundaries and

living them are two different things, and you deserve support for both.

Author's Note

On Research, Power, and Self-Respect

This book was not written in a vacuum.

This book is based on well-known research about burnout, emotional labor, people-pleasing, enmeshment, boundaries, and power in relationships. These challenges often show up for women, and anyone taught to put others first. The ideas here come from patterns found in clinical psychology, trauma research, and relationship studies. If you want to read more about the research, you can find a list of sources at the end of the book.

But this is not a textbook. It does not use the formal language of institutions that explains harm without having lived it. This book is not only based on research. It also comes from real-life experience, study, reflection, and the kind of understanding you get from living through it yourself.

The goal is not to diagnose you, label your experience, or make things feel cold and distant. Instead, this book aims to help you name what you already feel, notice patterns you may have lived with for years, and give you tools for setting boundaries that do not need anyone else's permission.

This book is here to educate, but it is not a substitute for therapy or professional help. If you are dealing with trauma, abuse, or a mental health crisis, please reach out to a qualified professional. You deserve more support than a book can offer on its own.

This book is, intentionally and without apology, about taking back what is yours: your self-trust, your personal authority, and your right to protect your peace without having to explain it to anyone.

That has always been the point.

Introduction

You didn't choose a book called *Boundaries Over Bullsh*t* because everything is perfect. You're here because, at some point, your peace was hijacked.

Maybe it was one too many "Do you have a sec?" requests at work. Maybe your family treats your time like it's community property. Maybe you have a friend who thinks your life revolves around their group chat. Or maybe you're just tired of always being the strong one, the responsible one, or the person who always says yes.

No matter what brought you here, one thing is clear: you're tired of carrying burdens that were never yours. Deep down, you already know this.

You feel it every time your stomach drops before answering a message. Every time you try to rest, your mind runs through everyone else's needs. You say "yes" even when every cell in your body is screaming, "Hell no."

You're not broken. **You're just burned out from years of being taught to put yourself last.**

We grow up in a world that praises over-giving. Be agreeable. Be accommodating. Be available. Be the good daughter, the dependable partner, the perfect employee, the reliable friend. We're taught to give up our time, energy, and peace just to be seen as "nice." If you didn't follow these rules, you were called selfish, difficult, or ungrateful.

So what happened? You adapted. You became quieter, smaller, less honest, less visible—less yourself.

Then one day, you woke up and wondered, *Why am I living my life for everyone except myself?*

That moment—when you feel quiet, tired, and fed up—is where your journey with boundaries starts.

This book gives you permission to stop shrinking, stop bending until you break, and stop accepting patterns you were conditioned to tolerate. Change won't happen overnight or perfectly, but it begins with one honest choice at a time.

Let's be clear: this isn't a simple "just say no" sunshine-and-rainbows guide. Boundaries can be messy, emotional, and uncomfortable. They bring up old wounds and challenge family rules, work expectations, and habits you built so long ago you forgot they were choices. And yes, sometimes they piss people off.

But boundaries can change everything, because they are one of the most powerful tools for self-respect you'll ever have.

Here's something people rarely say: **setting boundaries isn't about controlling others. It's about finally respecting yourself.**

In these pages, you'll unpack what brought you here, break out of guilt cycles, unlearn habits that kept you small, and build boundaries that work in real life—with your family, coworkers, partner, friends, kids, and even your phone. You'll get scripts, mindset shifts, and emotional tools for when pressure shows up. You'll learn the difference between a boundary, which protects you in the moment, and a standard, which defines who you are and what you allow into your life. And you'll learn how to use both.

By the end of this book, saying no won't feel wrong, speaking up won't feel like a threat, and choosing yourself won't feel like something that requires an apology.

We're not here to make you tougher or meaner, or to turn you into someone who doesn't care. **We're here to help you care about yourself, too.**

Are you ready? Good.

Before we can change anything, we need to talk about why you're so tired. Not the "I'm fine" version. **The real reason you feel drained isn't about laziness, weakness, or lack of discipline. It's about how much access others have had to your time, energy, and attention.**

In the next chapter, we'll name what's really been draining you, without shame and without pretending it happened overnight. Once you understand why, you'll stop blaming yourself—and that's when real change can start.

You're Not Tired — You're Overextended

You didn't become exhausted because you're weak. You became exhausted because you've been running other people's races with no finish line in sight.

The Moment You Realize Your Boundaries Are Paper-Thin

I knew my boundaries were shot when I spent my only day off helping a friend move—again. I was hauling boxes up two flights of stairs, sweating through my t-shirt, and pretending I wasn't hungry, while my phone kept buzzing with work messages and a voicemail from my mom asking why I hadn't responded to the new family group chat. By the end of the weekend, I felt completely empty—like a zombie carrying a to-do list, running on fumes and obligation.

That's when I realized my exhaustion wasn't about how hard I was working. **It was about** *access.* Too many people had a key to my time, energy, and attention, and I kept handing out copies without ever checking whether I had any left to give. Maybe you know that moment too. The one where you sit on the edge of your bed, stare at the wall, and wonder, *How the hell is everyone else doing life while I'm held together with caffeine and resentment?*

Here's the truth most people won't say out loud: you didn't end up here overnight, and there's nothing wrong with you. You were slowly taught to put yourself last. Every extra shift, every canceled plan, every time you ignored your own needs added up over time. You've been making promises to others at your own expense for years.

Your body is done accepting sacrifices. Now it wants to get paid.

Think of this chapter as a deep breath. It's your chance to finally name what's going on: boundary burnout. Stop blaming yourself for being weak or lazy. Boundary burnout happens when you take on too much, face too many demands, and don't have enough protection from other people's expectations for too long.

Boundary Burnout Is a Real Thing (And It's Not Your Fault)

Boundary burnout isn't a personal failure. It happens when you always put everyone else's comfort before your own. Maybe you keep saying yes to extra work because you can't stand to disappoint a coworker, or you show up for every family event while your own need for rest gets ignored. If you do this long enough, burnout doesn't just become a risk—it becomes your normal.

And it's not rare. It's everywhere.

Most of us learned early on that being easy to get along with was rewarded. Be the good kid. Be the team player. Help out without complaining. Put up with discomfort so others can stay comfortable. Over time, we started to believe our worth depended on how much we gave. As adults, the pressure only grew: work expects you to always be available, family wants you to drop everything, friends expect you to never say no, and even your phone demands your attention.

It's no surprise you feel drained and frustrated. Burnout isn't just about being tired. It's a slow, quiet breakdown that happens when you've been stretched too thin for so long that you forget what normal feels like. It might show up as irritability, resentment, brain fog, dreading messages, snapping at loved ones, or feeling overwhelmed by even small requests. This doesn't mean you're weak. It's your body's way of asking you to finally put yourself first.

Naming it isn't a weakness either. It's the first rebellious act against the cycle.

People-Pleasing Isn't Your Personality. It's Old Survival Software.

Here's what nobody told you growing up: the habits that kept you safe as a kid can become traps in adulthood.

As kids, most of us quickly learned the rules: don't upset anyone, don't argue, don't disappoint adults, and don't make things difficult. We got good at reading the room, watching people's faces, and changing ourselves to keep things calm. That wasn't weakness. It was self-preservation.

But those survival habits never really changed. They just kept going.

So now you're a grown woman replying to emails at 11pm, agreeing to things before you've thought them through, helping everyone else while you're drowning, and apologizing for existing in spaces you have every right to occupy. You say yes to commitments you'll resent. You constantly worry about upsetting someone. You lie about being busy because admitting you *just need rest* feels like a crime.

Living this way takes a bigger toll than you might think. For example, you might take on every extra project at work to avoid letting your boss down, but then you start dreading new tasks and resenting coworkers who set better boundaries. Over time, this leads to ongoing resentment, constant anxiety, and relationships that feel more like chores than choices. Deep down, there's a quiet sadness for the life you could have had if you'd known sooner that being liked isn't the same as being safe.

Take a quick look at your people-pleasing wiring:

- Do you agree to things you don't actually want to do?

- Does the word "no" make your stomach knot?

- Do you lie about being busy because you just need a damn break?

- Are you always the dependable one, even when it's costing you?

- Do you replay conversations, worried you upset someone?

- Are your needs always last on the list?

If several of those sound familiar, welcome. You're not broken; you've just been conditioned. There's a big difference between the two. Realizing this is the first step to letting go of people-pleasing software for good.

Emotional Labor: The Invisible Leak Draining You Dry

Have you ever spent time with someone and left feeling like you needed a nap, a drink, or even a week off? That's emotional labor—the invisible, unpaid work of managing other people's feelings, moods, crises, and expectations. Most of us do it all the time without realizing it has a price tag.

It's the coworker who vents to you daily but never once asks how you're doing. The friend who only calls when she has an emergency. The relative who treats you like their personal therapist, and then wonders why you seem distant. Sometimes people don't realize they're draining you. Sometimes they absolutely do. And sometimes they just don't give a damn—as long as you keep showing up with a smile and a solution.

Ask yourself:

- Who always leaves you feeling tired?

- Whose name on your screen makes your chest tighten?

- Which obligations drain you the fastest?

- Who just assumes you'll always say yes?

These aren't just complaints; they're a map. **Your energy is data. Your reactions are clues. Your fatigue is telling you exactly where your boundaries need reinforcement.**

You don't need permission to stop bleeding for people who won't bandage you. Managing someone else's emotions isn't proof of love. It's often a sign of old habits. Noticing where your energy leaks is how you finally stop hemorrhaging yourself dry.

Guilt and Anxiety Will Try to Hijack Your "No" — Let Them Go

If you've ever planned to say no and felt your body tense up, with your heart racing and your stomach tightening, and you want to over-explain, that's not weakness. That's your nervous system reacting to conflict as if it's dangerous. Your brain is doing what it learned to do, but those old experiences don't define you anymore.

Here's something people rarely say: **guilt doesn't mean you've done something wrong. It means you're trying something new and brave, something your old habits never prepared you for.** Think of guilt like muscle soreness after a new workout—it's uncomfortable, but it shows you're changing. Guilt means you're growing. It's not a stop sign. It's just your old self resisting change.

If your boundary only matters when everyone else agrees, it's not really a boundary. It's a negotiation.

Next time your "no" triggers a spiral, try this:

- **Breathe:** Four counts in, six counts out. Slow your body down before your mouth catches up.

- **Ground yourself:** "I can disappoint someone and still be a good person." Say it like you mean it.

- **Keep it simple:** "I can't take that on right now" is a complete sentence. You don't owe a backstory.

- **Let guilt throw its tantrum:** Feel it, acknowledge it, and let it pass. It will.

Every honest "no," even if it feels shaky, teaches your nervous system something new: protecting your peace isn't selfish, it's safe. The more you practice, the easier it gets. It doesn't get easier because it stops being hard. It gets easier because *you* become stronger.

When "Just Set Boundaries" Ignores Everything You Were Born Into

In some families, a boundary is seen as disrespect. In some cultures, it reads as betrayal. And for some people, depending on their identity, setting limits can feel genuinely risky in ways that go far beyond discomfort.

If you grew up hearing *"family comes first," "don't talk back,"* or *"good daughters always help"*—those messages didn't stay outside. They moved in. And now they're the voice in your head every time you consider putting yourself first.

Eldest daughters in immigrant families practically come out of the womb with a job description: caretaker, translator, peacemaker, and emotional anchor, all before they even know what boundaries *are*. LGBTQIA+ women face the extra challenge of their identity being a source of tension in family dynamics, making it even harder to ask for more space without it becoming *a big issue.* Many women were handed duties and responsibilities before they had any autonomy, and stepping back from those roles, even a little, can feel like breaking something sacred.

It's not. It's just new.

You might grieve the family dynamic you wish you had. The ease with which other people seem to move through relationships. The support you needed and didn't get. That grief is real, and it deserves space. But here's what's also true: **honoring your culture and honoring yourself are not mutually exclusive.** You can love your people deeply and still protect your well-being. You can show up for your community without disappearing in the process.

This isn't about tearing everything down. It's about choosing how much of yourself you're willing to set aside when you're with people you care about. Small boundaries matter. Each one you keep, even if it's imperfect or shaky, sends the same message:

I am a person, not a vending machine.

Stop Hinting. Start Saying It.

You know the dance. The heavy sigh. The *"I'm soooo busy"* hint dropped like a grenade. The passive comment. The slow fade. The ghost.

Honey, none of that shit works. It just makes you seem passive-aggressive, and the other person ends up confused. In the end, both of you feel resentful.

Avoiding direct conversations might feel safer at first, but that doesn't last. People who benefit from your silence rarely change unless you're clear with them. Hinting doesn't protect relationships; it wears them down. Resentment grows, misunderstandings pile up, and what started as a small issue quietly explodes into something neither of you saw coming. Friendships don't always end with a fight. Sometimes they just fade away because no one spoke up.

Here's the thing: people can't read your mind. Being clear isn't rude. It's actually one of the most respectful things you can do—both for them *and* for yourself.

A simple *"I can't take anything else on this week"* or *"I'm not available tonight"* isn't an attack. It's just information. It gives the other person something real to work with instead of leaving them guessing while you feel upset. Clear communication builds trust. It lets you be honest, without pretending everything is fine when it isn't.

You don't need a dramatic explanation or an airtight justification for your boundaries. Just state them clearly and calmly, and let them stand.

You don't owe anyone your backstory. **A boundary is complete the moment it's spoken.**

Reflection: Name the Leaks

Before you move on, sit with this for a minute. Think about the last month—the moments you felt drained, resentful, obligated, or just completely over it. The times you ignored what you needed to keep someone else comfortable. The situations where you handed over your time or energy and immediately regretted it.

Pick three of those moments. For each one, ask yourself:

- Where did I abandon myself in that moment?

- What boundary was missing, unclear, or straight-up ignored?

- What does this situation tell me about what I've been tolerating?

- What would the version of me I'm becoming do differently?

Write it down. Not because it's homework, but because the truth doesn't show up in just one moment. It shows up in patterns. You can't change what you haven't named.

Reminders

- **You're not exhausted because you're weak. You're exhausted because you were taught to ignore your own needs, and you've been doing it for a long time.**

- People-pleasing isn't kindness. It's often fear disguised as responsibility.

- Emotional labor is real, and it costs you, but you get to decide what you're willing to keep tolerating.

- **Boundary burnout is not a personal failure. It's a predictable result of chronic overextension.**

- Guilt is not a stop sign. It's a signal that you're finally doing something different.

- Cultural, family, and identity pressures are real, but they don't get to decide what you're allowed to protect.

- **Hinting leads to confusion. Being clear builds trust. Speak up.**

Burnout didn't happen because you're not enough. It happened because too many people had access to you, and no one, not even you, set real limits on how much they could take.

Awareness is where change begins. But awareness alone won't carry you through the moment someone's standing in front of you, asking for more than you have. That's where structure comes in.

In the next chapter, you'll learn a simple, repeatable framework to set boundaries in real life, even when emotions run high, words fail you, and the pressure to cave feels overwhelming.

Awareness names the problem. The next chapter hands you the blueprint to do something about it.

2

The Five-Step Boundary Blueprint

Clarity isn't selfish. It's the doorway your peace has been waiting to walk through.

When You Wish Boundaries Came With a User Manual

Picture this: you're at a family dinner, minding your business, eating your food, and managing your blood pressure. And then it happens. Your uncle, without missing a beat, launches into his favorite hobby: auditing your entire life. He questions your job, your relationship, your timeline, and your uterus.

Your face heats up. Your throat tightens. Your thoughts are all over the place. You want to respond differently this time—calm, clear, grounded—but the second someone challenges you, *poof*! Your mind goes blank. All that mental preparation disappears. Suddenly, you're caught off guard, scrambling for words you rehearsed a hundred times.

You might not hear this often, but boundaries aren't just for people who are naturally assertive, had perfect childhoods, or spent years in therapy. **Boundaries are a skill you can learn, practice, and improve over time.** The key isn't confidence. It's having a solid framework to rely on when life gets complicated. And as you know, life is usually messy.

That's exactly what this chapter offers you: a practical five-step blueprint built for real situations. The moments that challenge your boundaries rarely arrive when you're at your best. Instead, they pop up at family dinners, in parking lots, on group texts, and at 9pm on a Tuesday.

The Five-Step Boundary Blueprint

This section is the heart of the book: a practical, straightforward approach to the unpredictable, emotional moments of daily life. Keep it nearby and use it often. Come back to it when someone pushes your limits, and you feel overwhelmed. Here's the truth:

Boundary work isn't linear—and it was never meant to be.

Life changes. Relationships shift, your energy changes, old habits resurface, and people test your limits. Some days you'll feel steady and clear. You'll say what you mean, hold your boundary, and leave feeling like a new person. Other days, you might freeze, backtrack, say yes when you wanted to say no, and spend the next three hours replaying the whole conversation in your head, wondering why the words wouldn't come.

There is nothing wrong with you. When your inner critic storms in with guilt and self-doubt, or old fight-or-flight habits thunder through your body, remember that you're human, working through years of habits that once protected you. Progress moves in circles. It doesn't march in a straight line.

Perfect boundaries aren't the goal. What matters is that they're honest.

STEP 1: Clarify What You Actually Need (Not What You Were Conditioned to Want)

Most people don't struggle with boundaries due to weakness. They struggle because their needs were never centered in the first place.

Since childhood, most of us have learned to read the room and put others' needs before our own. Family expectations, cultural roles, work pressure, religious beliefs, the "strong woman" story that glorifies sacrifice, the idea that being busy means you're valuable, and the pressure from social media where everyone's life looks effortless—all of it adds up. After years of these messages, your own needs can start to feel like an inconvenience, something to apologize for, or something that never makes the priority list.

Your needs aren't indulgent. They help you function, stay balanced, and be present in your life. When your needs are ignored, your nervous system stays locked in a low-level tension, **that background hum of resentment and exhaustion you might mistake for your personality**. When your needs are met, your body relaxes. Boundaries become easier to keep. Resentment fades, and you show up with patience instead of feeling drained.

Take a notebook and write down five things that truly help you. They don't have to be big or life-changing. Often, the most important needs are the simplest: not having to pretend you're okay as soon as you wake up, time alone after being with others, being able to rest without explaining yourself, finishing a meal without guilt or distraction, or having space to process your feelings before you're expected to help someone else.

Then try this: write down one need in each area: emotional, physical, digital, and energetic. Don't worry about making a perfect list. Just notice what comes up. If you feel guilty as you write, don't judge yourself. That guilt is often just a sign of someone else's expectations that you never agreed to. Guilt doesn't mean your need is wrong. Usually, it means someone else's comfort was put ahead of your honesty for a long time.

Let your need stand on its own. You don't have to justify it to anyone, not even yourself. This is how you begin to honor what truly supports you.

STEP 2: *Spot Your Real Boundary Busters*

With your needs identified, the next challenge is recognizing who or what disrupts them. Boundary busters aren't always the obvious villains, but familiar interactions with people that blend into daily life. It's the friend who pops by unannounced and acts genuinely confused when you seem tired. The coworker who turns a "quick five-minute chat" into a forty-minute emotional download. The guilt-tripping relative who has mastered the art of making your "no" feel like a personal attack. The boss who sends messages at 10pm and calls it "just checking in." The group chat that never, ever sleeps. The partner who treats your time and energy like an open buffet. The neighbor who's been "borrowing" things since 2019 and hasn't returned a single one.

Sometimes the real boundary buster isn't another person; it's you. More specifically, it's the habits you developed to get by: overworking, over-explaining, replying right away, or saying yes before you even check if you have anything left to give. These weren't bad choices. They were ways to cope. They worked, until they didn't. Over time, they stopped feeling like choices and started to feel like just who you are.

But those habits aren't who you are. You have to notice them before you can change them.

Now make it personal. Jot down every person, situation, or habit that came to mind while reading this section. Don't edit yourself. Just put it all on the page. Then rate each one from 1 to 5, with 1 being a mild annoyance and 5 being total exhaustion. You'll quickly see patterns. The same people, situations, and requests will keep appearing at the top of your list. That's not a coincidence. That's useful information. **You can't protect what you haven't named.**

STEP 3: *Craft Boundaries That Actually Fit Your Life*

There's a lot of boundary advice online that sounds good until you try it. "Just say no." "Just cut them off." "Just leave." That might work if your life is simple, but most of us have more complicated situations. We deal with money issues, family history, cultural expectations, and relationships that aren't easy to walk away from. Setting a dramatic boundary might feel powerful at first, but it can be hard to keep up in real life.

Good boundaries need to fit your life: your culture, background, job, finances, past experiences, personality, and relationships. For example, one person might decide not to answer work emails after 6pm to protect their time, while someone else who needs flexible hours or has caregiving duties might set a different kind of limit for after-hours requests. What works for one person might not work for another. **Personalizing your boundaries makes them more likely to last.**

And don't underestimate the power of micro-boundaries, the small, everyday limits that most people overlook because they seem too minor to matter. Regularly practicing them is where real change happens, not because they're easier, but because you do them more often. Tech-free dinners. Not answering calls when you're resting. Muting a group chat that never stops. Not responding to every message the moment it arrives. Protecting your morning or evening routine like it's a meeting you can't cancel. These small limits build self-trust. And self-trust is exactly what makes the bigger, harder boundaries possible when the moment comes.

STEP 4: *Say It Like You Mean It (Even When Your Voice Shakes)*

Knowing your boundary is private work, but saying it out loud is what makes most people want to change the subject immediately.

It's normal to want to soften your words, hint, or put things off—no one wants conflict or to let loved ones down. But vague communication leaves room for misunderstanding and can lead to resentment. If you say, "I'm kind of busy" instead of, "I'm not available tonight," you hope the other person will understand. Most people won't. Then you feel frustrated that your hint was missed, and they feel confused. Clear language solves this quickly.

Your voice might shake the first few times. Your heart might race. You might replay the conversation later and wonder if you did it right. Remember, feeling uncomfortable doesn't mean you did something wrong. It means you're learning and growing. Trying something new always feels a bit awkward, and that's a normal part of making progress.

When You Need a Boundary Immediately

Sometimes you don't have the luxury of thinking through the perfect response. Someone is standing right in front of you, asking for something you don't have to give, and you need a sentence—just one clear sentence—that protects your space without starting a war.

In those moments, simple language is your best friend. You don't need a speech. You don't need a justification. You don't need to explain your childhood, your calendar, or your emotional bandwidth. You need one of these:

- "Thank you for thinking of me, but I can't take that on."

- "I'm not available for this."

- "That won't work for me."

Memorize these lines. Practice them in the mirror if you need to. These three sentences will help you through more awkward moments than you might expect because they're direct, respectful, and don't leave room for debate. If you need more scripts, check out Chapter 5: The Boundary Scripts Vault. You can jump ahead and come back when you're ready.

If you end a boundary with an explanation, it invites pushback. But a boundary that stands on its own leads to a very different conversation.

STEP 5: *Hold the Line. If You Break It, Repair It Stronger.*

Boundaries aren't battle lines. They are ongoing maintenance.

Here's the part nobody talks about enough: **setting the boundary is not the finish line. Holding it is.**

The real test of a boundary isn't other people—it's whether you're willing to stick to your limits when it's hard, when someone is upset, when you feel guilty, or when your old habits tell you it would be easier to give in. That hesitation doesn't mean you're wrong. It means you're changing. Change always feels awkward before it feels normal.

When someone crosses your boundary, your job isn't to prove they were wrong or make them feel guilty. Your job is to stay true to yourself. Restate your limit calmly, without giving a long explanation.

And when you slip up—because you will, and that's completely okay—don't treat it like a disaster. Maybe you said yes when you meant no. Maybe you answered without thinking. Maybe you let something go because you were tired and it was easier. None of this means you failed. It means you're human, and this work is tough. The goal was never perfection; it was progress. Returning to your boundary after a setback isn't starting over. It's how real change happens. **Self-trust isn't built only when you hold the line without hesitation; it's built when you come back to your boundary after you didn't.**

Write down the times you kept your boundary, even the small ones no one else noticed. Those moments matter more than you think. Progress comes from repeating these actions, not from putting pressure on yourself. Boundaries aren't proven just once—they're proven again and again, especially when life gets messy, and your old habits try to pull you back.

Reflection: Practice the Boundary Blueprint

Think of a recent time when you needed a boundary but didn't set one. Maybe you froze, said yes when you meant no, or hinted instead of being direct. Whatever happened, remember it without judging yourself. Just be curious about it.

Now ask yourself:

- What need was being ignored in that moment?

- What boundary would have honored it?

- What's one sentence you could use if that situation comes up again?

- How can you practice it before it does?

Write it down. Say it out loud. Practice it in your car on the way to work if you need to. Small changes bring peace. Small boundaries build strength. The more you practice before the pressure is on, the less likely you are to freeze when it happens.

Reminders

- You were never bad at boundaries. You were simply never taught a system that actually worked.

- Boundaries are a skill, not a personality trait. Skills can be learned.

- Naming your needs comes before setting limits. You can't protect what you haven't identified.

- Awareness reveals pressure points. Your energy and your reactions are data worth paying attention to.

- Personalized boundaries hold up under pressure. Generic scripts don't.

- Clear communication protects your energy and your relationships. Vague communication erodes both.

- Slipping doesn't mean starting over. It means recalibrating and continuing.

Boundaries don't fall apart in theory. They fall apart in real life, when you're tired, under pressure, when someone you care about is disappointed, or when your old habits are pulling you back. Now you have a framework for those times. It's not a magic fix, but it's a solid, repeatable process that gets stronger every time you use it.

In the next chapter, we'll use this blueprint in the places where it's tested the most: family, romantic relationships, friendships, parenting, work, and the spaces where your old roles are hardest to shake. This is where clarity meets your past, where the growing version of you meets the people and places that remember who you used to be.

Structure got you through the door. What comes next is where it really counts.

3

The Relationships That Know How to Get to You

Every relationship asks something of you. Boundaries decide what you're willing to give without losing yourself.

The Places That Pull You Back the Hardest

Having a framework is one thing. Once you start to understand your patterns, name your needs, and find the right words, it can feel more manageable. But nothing really prepares you for the moment you have to use these tools with the people who know you best.

It's much easier to set a boundary with a stranger or coworker than with someone who knows your history, understands how to make you give in, and has relied on your agreement for years. When someone close asks for something you don't want to give, all your preparation can suddenly feel out of reach.

Knowing what you need isn't the hard part. The real challenge is saying it to the people who have the most influence over you, like those who raised you, love you, depend on you, or live with you. Every relationship has its own unspoken rules and expectations about who you should be. As soon as you try to change even a small part of that, you'll feel pushback.

This is where the ideas from Chapter 2 get tested in your real relationships: family, parenting, work, friendships, romance, and roommates. Each brings its own kind of pressure and can pull you back into old roles. **Some boundaries are universal, but others need to fit the person you're dealing with. One thing stays the same: having boundaries doesn't break relationships. Pretending you don't need them breaks you.**

Family — Enmeshment, Obligation and the Weight of "How We've Always Done It"

Families are experts at this. One moment, you're a capable adult with your own life. The next, you're back to being the helper, crisis manager, mediator, or emotional punching bag, wondering how it happened and why it still catches you off guard.

In many families, especially those that are collectivist, traditional, or multigenerational, individuality can fade into the background. Your time becomes something everyone shares. Your energy is expected to be available. Your needs might become negotiable or even ignored. These beliefs are often tied to love, which makes them harder to challenge. You're not up against a villain—you're dealing with a system that existed before you and that everyone believes is normal.

This is called enmeshment, and it usually doesn't show up as open conflict. It grows through roles you never chose, like being the translator, the peacekeeper, or the one who organizes every holiday and handles every crisis without anyone checking on you. These roles turn into expectations, expectations become obligations, and over time, those obligations can feel like your whole identity.

Families also hand down invisible emotional contracts—unspoken rules about who owes what to whom. Phrases like "After everything I've done for you," "You're the only one who can handle this," or "That's just how our family works" aren't neutral. They're pressure disguised as tradition, making it hard to say no without feeling guilty. **Exhaustion isn't devotion. It's self-abandonment disguised as duty. That lie can build up for years without anyone naming it.**

What actually helps is being clear without apologizing. You can offer help for a set amount of time. You can say no to financial requests that go beyond your limits. You can ask for advance notice before last-minute demands. You can love your family and still set limits on your time and peace. These things aren't in conflict, even if it feels that way. If culture or tradition is used as pressure, remember: if a family expects you to disappear to keep the peace, that's not culture. That's control.

Over-explaining opens the door to negotiation. Your boundary doesn't need to be debated. It just needs to be stated clearly and held. Small changes, like limiting calls, taking real breaks during visits, or scheduling time together instead of always being available, can protect your energy without damaging the relationship. If you say yes too quickly and start to feel resentful, you can reset. Admit you overcommitted and make a change. Most people adjust faster than your guilt does.

Sometimes, softer boundaries aren't enough. If your time, energy, or money keeps getting drained, setting a firmer limit isn't disloyal. It's self-preservation. For big shared responsibilities like caregiving or finances, written agreements aren't cold. They provide clarity that protects everyone, including the relationship, by removing confusion before resentment builds.

You don't heal by staying loyal to the role that once broke you.

Parenting — Modeling What You Wish Someone Had Shown You

Parenting is one of the hardest places to set boundaries because the cultural message is that good parents should be relentlessly selfless, endlessly patient, and always available. This story isn't true—it leaves real parents exhausted, guilty, and worn out, and it doesn't deliver the results it promises.

Kids don't need a superhero. They need a parent who shows them how to manage their own emotions and needs. What often surprises parents is that the boundaries you set for yourself are some of the most valuable parenting tools you have.

When your child hears you say, *"I need a few minutes to reset,"* and sees you actually take that time, they learn that it's okay to name and respect needs. If you say, *"I'll help you after I finish this,"* without guilt, they see that other people's needs don't erase your own. When they watch you take a walk alone, close a door, or say no to something that would drain you, they're learning a skill you want them to have as adults. You're not holding back from them—you're showing them that emotional limits are normal and safe, not something to be ashamed of.

It also means you can stop performing availability you don't actually have. *"I need a minute." "I need some quiet." "Let's talk about this tomorrow when I can actually listen"*—these aren't rejections. They're honest communication from someone who knows their own limits, which is exactly what you want your kid to grow up doing.

In co-parenting and blended families, clarity matters even more because the stakes for confusion are higher. Two households don't need identical rules. They need adults who communicate predictably and keep their disagreements out of the children's line of sight. That means getting aligned on the essentials—schedules, discipline, how you speak about each other—and sticking to those agreements even when the relationship between the adults is hard.

Teenagers will test every limit you set. That's not failure on your part—that's developmental biology doing exactly what it's supposed to do. Their job at that stage is to push toward independence. Your job is to stay steady, keep the structure intact, and not take the pushing personally. When you lose your cool—and you will, because you're a person, not a saint—you repair it. You name what happened, you reset the tone, and you model exactly the accountability you want them to practice. That repair, done simply and without drama, teaches more than the original limit ever could. Kids remember the comeback more than the crack.

Work — Protecting Your Time, Energy and Sanity in an Always-On Culture

Modern workplaces are good at making everything seem urgent, even when it's not. Remote work has especially blurred the line between being available and just living your life. Many people now answer emails while reheating dinner and think that's normal.

Burnout at work doesn't happen all at once. It builds up slowly—one after-hours message answered, then another, until it's expected. One "quick favor" taken on, then another, until it's just part of your job. The work grows to fill any space you don't protect, and by the time you notice, exhaustion feels normal.

Professional boundaries aren't about attitude. They're about making expectations clear. When boundaries are missing, conflict grows because unspoken expectations create resentment much faster than any honest conversation.

"I'm at capacity. What should I deprioritize?" shifts the conversation from your limitation to shared problem-solving. *"I'm unavailable after 6pm. I'll respond tomorrow"* communicates a limit without requiring an explanation or an apology. *"I*

20

realized I overcommitted. Let's revisit the timeline." is honest and professional without being defensive. These aren't declarations of war. They're sentences that protect your time while keeping the relationship functional.

Your phone can help you set boundaries or make it harder to maintain them. How you set it up matters more than your intentions. Using Do Not Disturb, calendar focus blocks, clear status updates, and auto-replies after hours isn't antisocial—it's structure. Structure at work lowers stress by making expectations clear before frustration builds.

If people keep ignoring your boundaries even after you've been clear, don't just work harder or explain more. Instead, reinforce your boundary, document things if needed, and consider whether the environment is the real problem—not your effort. **Your job can be replaced. Your well-being cannot. Protect that shit.**

(Need scripts for specific work issues? Chapter 5 has you covered.)

Friendships — When Connection Starts Feeling Like Caretaking

Friendships should make you feel lighter. That's the point—having someone who knows you, chooses you, and makes everyday life easier. But sometimes the balance changes so gradually that you don't notice until every conversation feels like emotional work.

If every conversation is about their crisis, their drama, or their need for reassurance, and there's no space for your needs, that's not real connection. That's taking. The hard truth is that some friendships were built when you didn't have boundaries. You were always available, always helping. When you start setting limits, some friendships will struggle. It's not because you stopped caring, but because the relationship depended on your unlimited availability, and that's what's actually expiring.

The signs aren't always obvious. Maybe you feel uneasy when their name pops up, or relieved when plans are canceled. After talking, you might feel drained instead of energized. Pay attention to these feelings—they're telling the truth, even if the friendship feels complicated.

Healthy friendships don't just survive limits. They're protected by them. *"I care about you, but I don't have the bandwidth for a heavy conversation today"* is something a real friend can hear and respect. *"I can't lend money right now"* doesn't have to end a friendship. *"I can't make it this week. Let's plan for next"* is not abandonment. These are words someone uses when they value the relationship enough to show up to it honestly, instead of performing availability they don't have.

Eventually, explaining turns into performing. Once you've said what you need to say, let your actions speak for you. If your boundaries keep getting ignored, you don't have to explain more. Change your behavior—say no more often, keep conversations shorter, or create some distance. If the friendship can't handle you having needs, that says a lot about what it was built on. **It's normal to mourn the end of your connection. Some friendships end not because you stopped caring, but because you started caring about yourself.**

That's not cold. That's growth.

Romance — Loving Deeply Without Disappearing

You can love someone with your whole heart and still need to be a separate person. Those two things aren't in conflict, but in close relationships, they can start to feel that way.

Closeness without independence isn't intimacy. It's fucking suffocation disguised as devotion. This usually happens slowly. Maybe you gave up a hobby because it took time away from your partner, let a friendship fade because it made them uncomfortable, or felt like you can't fully relax in a relationship that should feel safe. What starts as closeness can turn into pressure that neither of you meant, but both of you notice.

Having space in a relationship isn't the same as pulling away. It's what allows closeness to last. When you have time to reset, think, and reconnect with yourself, you return with more patience, presence, and the qualities that make the relationship strong. Without that space, resentment can quietly grow between who you pretend to be and who you really are.

If you're afraid to ask your partner for time alone because you're unsure how they'll react, that's a sign the relationship is unbalanced and worth looking at. Saying, *"I recharge alone. It helps me be better with you,"* is honest and healthy. *"I love us, and I also need solo time to reset,"* isn't a threat. *"Let's pause this conversation and come back to it tomorrow,"* isn't avoidance. It's choosing to respond thoughtful*ly, which is what good communication looks like.

Digital and privacy boundaries matter here, too. Don't read each other's messages without permission. Have phone-free meals. Agree on what you share on social media and what stays private. Respect a closed door. These aren't about hiding things—they're about mutual respect, which is the foundation of trust.

Conflict is inevitable in every close relationship. Boundaries aren't about avoiding it—they're about knowing when to step back before saying something you'll regret. **Space isn't the same as distance. Space lets you breathe.**

Roommates — Because Nobody Warned You About the Dishes

Nothing exposes incompatibility quite like figuring out who refills the toilet paper.

Roommate conflicts usually don't start with big fights. They build up from small annoyances that no one talks about, like a dish left in the sink, noise at the wrong time, or chores that always fall to the same person. Over time, the tension grows until everyone is unhappy. Most of this can be prevented, since it comes from assumptions, not bad intentions. People grow up with different habits and ideas about what's clean, quiet, or polite. Having direct conversations early can prevent months of silent frustration.

"I need quiet after 10pm" is not a demand. It's information. *"Can we give each other a heads-up before overnight guests?"* prevents the kind of situation that poisons a living space for weeks. *"I've noticed I'm handling the dishes most days. Can we rotate more evenly?"* addresses the pattern without assigning blame. These aren't dramatic confrontations. They're five-minute conversations that save five months of resentment.

Simple systems help everyone. Rotating chores, setting quiet hours, and being clear about shared supplies and guests create the structure needed to live together well. If problems keep happening even after you've talked about them, it's time to change the system. Hold a house meeting, make new agreements, involve the landlord, or think about moving out. Leaving a living situation that makes you unhappy isn't failure. It's taking care of yourself.

You're not high-maintenance. You're protecting your peace. There's a difference.

Reflection: Where Is the Weight Heaviest?

You've just walked through six different relationship landscapes. Before you move on, sit with this for a minute.

Pick the one that's sitting with you most right now—the section you read more slowly, the example that hit a little too close, the relationship where you feel the most overextended.

You don't have to work through all of them at once. The one that pulled your attention is the right starting point.

For that relationship, ask yourself:

- Where does my energy drop the fastest?

- What expectation feels the most unfair or the most exhausting to keep meeting?

- What boundary, even a small one, would give me the most immediate relief?

- What's one sentence—clear, honest, and something I could actually say—that I could practice this week?

Write it down. Say it out loud. You deserve to hear yourself speak up after carrying all of this quietly.

Every time you speak up for a boundary, you challenge the part of you that learned to stay silent. You don't have to twist yourself to make others comfortable anymore. This is where that stops.

Reminders

- Relationships are where the blueprint gets its hardest real-world test, and where it matters most.

- **Family boundaries aren't betrayal. They're the conditions under which you can keep showing up without disappearing.**

- Parenting with limits isn't selfish—it's the most direct way to teach your children what you wish you'd learned.

- Work boundaries aren't unprofessional. They're what sustainable performance actually requires.

- Friendships require reciprocity, not emotional caretaking.

- **You can love someone completely and still need to be a whole person. Those two things aren't in conflict.**

- Nobody figures out the roommate rules on their own. Have the conversation.

Relationships don't end because of boundaries. They fall apart when boundaries are missing. That's when resentment grows where honesty should be, when roles turn into obligations, and when people stop seeing each other as individuals and start acting like they're just filling a role.

You've just done the hardest relationship work in this book. You've looked at the people and situations where your boundaries are tested most, and you're starting to see them clearly, maybe for the first time.

But there's one area where boundaries fade faster and more quietly than anywhere else. There's no conversation or direct pressure—just constant, subtle access that your mind gets used to so slowly you barely notice.

Your digital world.

In the next chapter, we talk about how always-on technology trains you to stay alert, available, and emotionally on call around the clock, and how to reclaim your attention, your time, and your peace without guilt or apology.

Boundaries aren't just about relationships. They're also about who and what gets your attention.

4

You Are Not a Hotline — Reclaiming Your Attention

You don't owe every ping, buzz, or notification a piece of your life. Your attention is a privilege — not a public utility.

The Phone You Never Agreed to Be On Call For

You put your phone down for forty-five minutes. Maybe you took a shower, ate a meal without taking a photo, or just sat quietly for a moment without being available to anyone.

Then you pick it back up.

When you pick up your phone again, you see 37 texts, 14 notifications, and two group chats that kept going while you were away. Someone noticed you read a message and feels a bit upset. Three work emails arrived after hours and are waiting for your reply. Meanwhile, a friend asks, "You okay??" just because you were quiet for a while.

You weren't gone. You were just human for forty-five minutes.

This is an important boundary that people don't talk about much. Digital overwhelm is now part of everyday life, and we often accept it without question. But just because it's common doesn't mean it's harmless. Paying attention to your boundaries and protecting them matters for your well-being.

We've been taught that always being reachable means you're responsible, that quick replies show you care, and that being quiet, even for a short time, can seem like rejection. These beliefs don't announce themselves. Instead, they show up as anxiety when your phone lights up, frustration when someone wants a quick reply you can't give, and the tired feeling of always trying to keep up with conversations you never asked for. The emotional effort behind every notification is real, even if each one seems small. Over time, it adds up.

You're a person, not a hotline. Putting your real limits before being constantly available online is important for your mental health. This chapter will help you reclaim your attention and set boundaries that work for you.

Group Chats: The Connection That Quietly Became a Commitment

Group chats are a great way to stay connected. They keep inside jokes going, help with plans, and make you feel like you belong, even from a distance. But sometimes, that feeling shifts.

At some point, and you probably know this feeling, a group chat stops feeling like connection and starts to feel like work. You step away for three hours and return to 94 messages, a conversation that ended without you, and the stress of wondering if you should reply or if it's too late. You might feel rude for not keeping up, guilty for wanting some quiet, and a little behind in your friendships.

Group chats can feel like family, with unspoken rules and hidden expectations. There's usually at least one person who takes it personally if you don't reply quickly. It's as if there's a social contract everyone is supposed to follow, even though no one agreed to it. If you go quiet or mute the chat, you might feel guilty, even if it doesn't really make sense.

Remember, **your value isn't measured by how fast you reply.** Wanting to move at your own pace, instead of keeping up with notifications, doesn't make you cold or a bad friend. It just means you want to be present when you're there, not just physically present. The chat will still be there. The friendship will last. The people who matter will understand, especially if you let them know what's going on.

You can handle this with simple words and no drama. For example, saying, *"Muting this chat for a bit. Message me directly if something's urgent"* sets clear, respectful expectations. *"I'm responding more slowly these days so I can actually be present when I do"* is honest and doesn't apologize. You're not abandoning anyone, and you don't have to give the chat a version of yourself that isn't real right now. Being honest about your limits is more respectful than disappearing or pretending to be involved when you're not.

Muting, Blocking, and Unfollowing: The Self-Respect Nobody Talks About

Let's talk about the social shame that comes with the quiet ways of protecting yourself online.

People say blocking is dramatic, unfollowing is petty, and muting is passive-aggressive. Soft-blocking barely has a name, but it still has a reputation. The message is clear: using these tools to manage your digital life is often seen as an overreaction, as if you have to explain yourself.

It doesn't.

You know what it's like to unfollow someone you know in real life. There's a whole internal debate first: *will they notice? Will they say something? Is this even worth it?* All these questions come up before you do anything. And if you go through with it, the guilt still shows up, even if it was the right choice. That guilt is just the noise in your head, always telling you that your comfort comes last.

Spoiler alert: it doesn't.

Here's the important difference: avoidance means disappearing because something feels uncomfortable. Healthy disengagement is stepping back because the interaction always drains you, your limits aren't respected, or the relationship feels truly unsafe. These are not the same thing, even if they look similar from the outside.

Avoidance is disappearing because you feel uncomfortable. Healthy disengagement is stepping back from interactions that drain you or ignore your limits. The difference is your reason: muting to protect your energy is self-care, but muting to avoid a hard conversation is something to consider.

If you've spoken up at least once and nothing changed, stepping back isn't avoidance. It's wisdom. Tools like muting, blocking, unfollowing, restricting, archiving, or leaving the chat exist for this reason.

Using these tools isn't an overreaction. It's self-care.

When People Treat Your Online Presence Like Shared Property

Digital boundaries aren't just about handling too many messages or notifications. Sometimes the pressure is more specific and personal.

You post a photo and a relative comments on your body. A friend tags you in something without asking, in a context where you didn't want to be visible. Someone notices you posted a story but didn't reply to their message, and brings it up like evidence. An ex tracks everything you share. A coworker screenshots your personal post to discuss it with someone else. You share something vulnerable, and it gets used in a conversation you weren't part of.

All these examples have the same problem: just because people can see you online doesn't mean they have permission to comment or interact however they want. Being accessible doesn't mean you're always available. Being online doesn't mean you're open to everything. Posting something doesn't mean you've agreed to every possible response. **Your digital presence is like a window, not an open door.**

This is true for dating too, and it's important to say it clearly. In online dating, things can move so fast that it creates a false sense of urgency and closeness before trust has time to grow. If someone pushes for quick replies, asks for personal details before you're ready, or uses their impatience as proof of how much they like you, that's not chemistry. **Pressure isn't chemistry. Urgency isn't affection. Control isn't connection.** Your pace isn't a problem; it shows how you move through the world, and the right person will respect that instead of trying to change it.

Reclaiming Your Attention Without Burning It All Down

You don't need to do a dramatic digital detox. You don't have to delete your apps, announce a break from social media, or disappear to make this work. Small, steady changes in how you use technology will help more in the long run than any big gesture that you can't keep up.

The goal isn't to use less technology, but to take back control of your attention. Right now, most people let technology decide when they engage, giving up that control. Taking it back is at the heart of digital boundaries.

Taking back your attention means checking messages when you want to, not every time something pops up. It means keeping your phone out of the bedroom so your mornings and nights belong to you, not your inbox. It also means turning off notifications for apps that don't need your immediate attention, which, if you're honest, is most of them. Try setting aside parts of your day without devices—not as punishment, but as recovery time your brain needs. Meals, walks, the first hour in the morning, and the last thirty minutes before sleep are good times for this because they're natural transitions, and transitions are the easiest times to build new habits.

If you've been too available and want to reset expectations, you can say, *"I've been stretched too thin, so I'm responding more slowly from now on."* That's all most people need. How others react will show how they value your time.

Reflection: Your Digital Boundaries Audit

Take five minutes to think about these questions. You don't need a perfect plan—just notice what's really draining you.

Ask yourself:

- Which apps or chats consistently leave you more drained than when you opened them?

- Whose messages trigger anxiety before you've even read them?

- When do notifications feel like demands rather than communication?

- What is one small, doable change this week that could give your attention more room to breathe?

Write it down, and then take action before you talk yourself out of it.

Digital boundaries aren't about disappearing. **They're about choosing to be present instead of feeling pressured.**

Reminders

- **Notifications aren't emergencies, and your response time doesn't prove your care, loyalty, or worth.**

- Group chats have rules nobody agreed to. You can slow down the pace without stepping away from the people.

- **Muting, blocking, and unfollowing are tools, not character flaws. Use them without feeling guilty.**

- Being visible isn't the same as being available. A post isn't an invitation. A story isn't a conversation.

- **Urgency isn't affection, whether online or in person.**

- You don't need a big gesture to reclaim your attention. Small, purposeful choices make the difference—not desperate actions.

You've done a lot of internal work in these four chapters: naming the problem, building a framework, applying it to relationships, and now reclaiming your digital space. But knowing all this doesn't help when someone is right in front of you or texting you, and you need the right words.

That's what comes next.

Chapter 5 is the Boundary Scripts Vault. It gives you the exact words for the moments that are hardest to handle. Boundaries don't fail because of a lack of intention. They fail when you don't have the words you need.

Let's make sure you always have something steady to count on.

5

The Boundary Scripts Vault

Your voice becomes powerful the moment you stop using it to keep everyone comfortable and start using it to keep yourself whole.

Your Cheat Sheet for the Moments That Make Your Stomach Drop

Scripts don't help because they sound clever. **They work because pressure often hits before you have time to think.** When someone is waiting for your answer, you need something steady to hold onto so you don't just say yes by default.

Maybe someone is in front of you, on your phone, or across the table at a family dinner. Your mind goes blank, your heart races, and you can't think clearly. This chapter is for those moments.

These scripts aren't supposed to sound perfect or rehearsed. They're here to help you when pressure hits and you can't find your words. Being clear is better than being clever, so each script is short, direct, and works even if your voice shakes. Scripts don't make you stiff. They help you feel prepared.

Read through all the scripts. Mark the ones that feel most urgent. Practice the ones that make you uncomfortable, since those are likely the ones you need most.

At Work — Protecting Your Time Without Burning Bridges

Feeling anxious about work boundaries is normal. You need your job, you care about your reputation, and being a team player matters to you. So when someone asks for a quick favor at the end of the day or schedules a meeting over your lunch break again, saying no can feel risky. But it isn't. What you really can't afford is losing your energy and focus by always saying yes.

When someone asks you to take on more than you can handle:

- *"My current workload won't allow me to take this on without affecting other priorities—which would you like me to deprioritize?"*

- *"I want to help. Can we talk about what gets moved to make room for this?"*

- *"I'm at capacity right now. I can pick this up next week if the timeline allows."*

When after-hours messages become the expectation:

- *"I'll review this first thing tomorrow morning."*

- *"I've noticed more after-hours requests lately—can we revisit availability expectations as a team?"*

- *"I'm offline after 6pm. I'll get back to you in the morning."*

When your boss is the one pushing past your limits:

This situation needs its own scripts because there's a real power imbalance. You can be direct and still stay professional.

- *"I want to make sure I'm delivering quality work. Can we talk about realistic timelines for this?"*

- *"I can absolutely prioritize this—I'll need to let you know what I'm moving to make it happen."*

- *"I want to flag that I'm approaching my capacity. I'd rather tell you now than deliver something undercooked."*

When you need to reverse a commitment you already made:

- *"I said yes too quickly on that. I've looked at my workload, and I need to adjust—here's what I can realistically do."*

- *"I realized I overcommitted. Can we revisit the scope or timeline?"*

With Family — Love Without Losing Yourself

You know your family. You know which phrases trigger your guilt spiral, which relatives push back hardest, and which conversations feel like emotional ambushes regardless of how they start. These scripts are built for those complicated interactions.

When you need to set limits on availability:

- *"I love staying connected, but I need some downtime after work before I can be fully present. I'll reach out when I'm recharged."*

- *"I'm not available for calls right now, but I'll get back to you soon."*

- *"I need to keep visits shorter for a while. It's not about you. I'm protecting my energy."*

When unsolicited advice or criticism shows up:

- *"I appreciate that you care. I need to work through this on my own first."*

- *"I hear you. I'm going to handle it my way."*

- *"I'm not looking for feedback on this—I just wanted to share."*

When guilt-tripping language appears:

Phrases like "after everything I've done for you" or "if you really cared" are meant to make your boundary feel like a betrayal. Don't take them as a reason to explain yourself more. Take them as a sign to stand firm.

- *"I understand this is hard for you. My answer is still the same."*

- *"I know we see this differently. I'm not going to change my mind on this one."*

- *"I love you, and I'm not going to argue about this."*

When you need to decline a request:

- *"I'm not in a position to help with that right now."*

- *"That doesn't work for me."*

- *"I can't take that on."*

Full stop. You don't need to explain further.

When culture, tradition, or obligation is used as leverage:

- *"I can honor our family and still have limits. Those aren't opposites."*

- *"This is what I need. I'm not asking permission."*

Space doesn't weaken family bonds. It actually helps keep them strong.

Friends — When Loyalty Starts Feeling Like a Full-Time Job

You care about this person, but sometimes you feel dread when you see their name on your screen. Both feelings can exist at the same time, and this section is here to help with that tension.

When someone asks for more than you have:

- *"I care about you, and I don't have the bandwidth for a heavy conversation today. Can we talk tomorrow?"*

- *"I'm not able to lend money right now."*

- *"I wish I could help with that. My schedule is full."*

- *"I can't make it this week. Let's plan something for next month."*

Healthy friendships change as expectations change. If things start to feel unbalanced, honest communication gives you a chance to reset:

- *"I've realized I've been overextending and I need to pull back a bit. I want our friendship to feel mutual."*

- *"I need our friendship to have more balance. I care about you too much to let resentment build."*

When plans need to be canceled or shortened:

- *"Something came up, and I need to cancel. I'll reach out to reschedule when things settle."*

- *"I need to cut today short. I'm more drained than I expected."*

When someone pushes back on a limit you've already set:

- *"I hear you. My boundary stays the same."*

- *"We can disagree on this and still be friends. But I'm not changing my answer."*

In Romantic Relationships — Intimacy That Doesn't Require Disappearing

The following scripts are for those times when intimacy gets complicated, like when you need space, time to cool down, or a real talk about a pattern you haven't named yet.

When you need space without it becoming an argument:

- *"I recharge when I have time alone. It helps me show up better with you. It's not about us."*

- *"I need some solo time this weekend. I'll reach out after I've had time to reset."*

- *"I love you, and I also need time that's just mine. Both of those things are true."*

When a conversation needs to pause before it gets worse:

- *"I want to talk about this, and I need a break first. Can we come back to it in an hour?"*

- *"I'm too activated right now to have a productive conversation. Give me some time to reset."*

- *"I reacted because I felt overwhelmed. I need to step away and come back when I can really listen."*

When privacy or digital limits need to be stated:

- *"I need us to have an agreement about going through each other's phones. That's a line for me."*

- *"I'd like us to check in before posting photos of each other."*

- *"I need phone-free time together. Can we make that a regular thing?"*

When you need to address a pattern, not just a moment:

- *"This isn't about one incident. I need us to address how this keeps showing up."*

- *"I've noticed a pattern I want to talk about. When X keeps happening, I feel Y, and I need Z."*

Roommates — For the Conversations You've Been Avoiding

No one tells you that living with someone takes almost as much communication as loving them. You might go weeks without a real conversation but still share every part of daily life, so unspoken issues build up quickly. There's the quiet resentment of doing things alone, the worry about bringing something up, and the stress of keeping score without meaning to. You're not looking for a perfect roommate, just a workable setup. That starts with saying what you need before it turns into a conflict.

When expectations need to be set or reset:

- *"I need quiet after 10pm—is that something we can agree on?"*

- *"Can we talk about the dishes? I've been handling them most days, and it's starting to wear on me."*

- *"I'd like us to give each other a heads-up before bringing overnight guests. Is that reasonable?"*

When a shared responsibility has fallen lopsided:

- *"I've noticed I've been handling most of the cleaning. Can we put together a rotation?"*

- *"The bills have been inconsistent. Can we set up a system so it's not on me to track every month?"*

When something has already gone sideways:

- *"I should have said something sooner. Here's what I need going forward."*

- *"This has been building for a while, and I'd rather address it now than let it get worse."*

You Don't Owe Strangers an Explanation Either

People often forget that boundaries aren't just for close relationships. They also apply to the coworker you barely know who asks personal questions, the acquaintance who expects favors, and the person at a party who asks about things that are none of their business.

When someone asks something too personal:

- *"I prefer to keep that private."*

- *"I'm not going to get into that."*

- *"That's not something I talk about."*

When someone makes an unwanted comment about your body, choices, or life:

- *"I didn't ask for feedback on that."*

- *"I'm not interested in discussing this."*

- *"Let's change the subject."*

When you need to exit a conversation that's gone sideways:

- *"I'm going to step away from this conversation."*

- *"I don't have more to add here."*

- *"I need to move on."*

The Hardest Scripts — For the Moments Nobody Prepares You For

Some boundaries are respected after you state them once. Others get tested repeatedly by people who are hoping you'll give in, soften, or forget what you said. This section is for those times—when you've already set a limit, the relationship is strained, and you still need words that hold without making things worse. These scripts won't make those moments easy, but they'll help you get through them.

When someone violates a boundary you've already clearly stated:

This is where repeating yourself matters. Don't add new arguments or explanations. Just calmly repeat your limit as many times as needed. New explanations invite more debate, but repetition shows your boundary isn't up for discussion.

- *"I already addressed this. My answer is the same."*

- *"We've talked about this. Nothing has changed on my end."*

- *"I'm not going to keep explaining this. The boundary stands."*

When someone says "you've changed" as an accusation:

They're right. That's the point.

- *"You're right. I have."*

- *"I'm not who I was. This is who I am now."*

- *"Yes, and this is what that looks like."*

When you need to ask for more time before committing:

These are some of the most underused scripts out there, and also some of the most powerful.

- *"Let me think about that and get back to you."*

- *"I need a day to check my capacity. I'll let you know tomorrow."*

- *"I don't make commitments on the spot anymore. I'll follow up."*

When you need to decline a social obligation without a performance:

- *"I'm not going to be able to make it."*

- *"That doesn't work for me."*

- *"I'm going to sit this one out."*

You don't need to explain yourself. Seriously.

When someone pushes back, and you feel yourself starting to fold:

This is the moment when your old habits will push you to give in, over-explain, soften, or compromise in ways that don't serve you. Don't give in to that urge.

- *"I understand you're disappointed. My answer is still no."*

- *"I hear you. Nothing changes on my end."*

- *"This isn't up for debate."*

None of these are easy to say at first. Some won't feel natural until you've tried them several times. That's normal. You're not just learning new words—you're also unlearning the habit of managing everyone else's reactions. Keep these scripts nearby. Use them, even if it feels awkward. **An imperfect boundary still works. A swallowed one doesn't.**

When You Break Your Own Boundary — Repair Without the Shame Spiral

It will happen. You'll say yes when you mean no, stay too long, or agree before you've had time to think. That doesn't mean you failed. It just means you're human, and your old habits kicked in before your new ones.

Before you try to fix things, check in with yourself. Where did you let yourself down? Was it when you said yes, stayed silent, or explained too much? What was behind that moment—anxiety, guilt, or wanting to avoid conflict? Repair starts with noticing these things, not blaming yourself.

Then correct course. Simply, directly, and without drama.

- *"I said yes too quickly. I need to make an adjustment—here's what I can actually do."*

- *"I've thought about it more, and I'm not able to follow through on that."*

- *"I spoke from habit, not from what I actually have available. Let me reset."*

- *"I need to update the plan. I'm stepping back from that commitment."*

The goal isn't to be perfect with your boundaries. The goal is to notice when you slip, fix it, and move on without turning it into a big emotional event. Your body remembers when you mess up, but it also remembers when you repair. **Each time you fix a mistake, you build more self-trust than you lost.**

Speaking Up in Groups — You Weren't Put in That Room to Stay Quiet

Group settings bring their own pressure. There's the strong personality who takes over, the meeting that ends before you can speak, or the social situation where everyone seems fine with something that bothers you. Staying quiet feels like the path of least resistance until you're driving home fuming about what you didn't say.

When you need to hold the floor or re-enter a conversation:

- *"I'd like to finish my thought."*

- *"I want to come back to what I was saying before we moved on."*

- *"I have something to add before we close this."*

When someone else is being talked over:

- *"Let them finish."*

- *"I'd like to hear what she was saying."*

When you're uncomfortable with the direction of a conversation:

- *"I'm not comfortable with where this is going."*

- *"I'm going to opt out of this one."*

- *"This isn't a conversation I want to be part of."*

When you disagree, and you're going to say so:

- *"I see this differently."*

- *"I want to offer a different perspective."*

- *"I don't agree with that and here's why."*

These statements communicate confidence without aggression. They protect your voice while maintaining respect for others.

These statements show confidence without being aggressive. They help you speak up while still respecting others. The first time you use one in a group, it might feel huge. Your voice might shake, and you might second-guess yourself later. Do it anyway. That's not failure. That's you growing. The second time is easier, and by the third time, it feels natural.

Reflection: The Conversation You've Been Putting Off — Start Here

Take a few minutes with this before you move on.

Think about the scripts in this chapter that made you uncomfortable—the ones you read and thought, I could never say that. Those are probably the ones you need most. Choose one situation, one person, or one conversation you've been avoiding or dreading.

Ask yourself:

- What do I need to say? What's the first sentence?

- What am I afraid will happen if I say it—and is that fear based on evidence or on old wiring?

- What's the actual cost of staying silent one more time?

Write down the sentence. Say it out loud, even if it's just to yourself. Notice how your body reacts when you hear your own voice say something clear. That reaction matters. **Every time you speak a boundary, you shift your identity from someone who just goes along with everything to someone who is clear.**

Reminders

- Scripts don't make you rigid. They prepare you for the moments when pressure arrives faster than clarity.

- **Clear language beats clever lines every time. Short, direct, and honest is the way to go.**

- You don't owe anyone an explanation for a boundary you've already stated.

- **"You've changed" is not an accusation worth defending. It's a compliment worth owning.**

- The broken-record approach works because it removes the debate. Repetition without escalation is a complete strategy.

- **Asking for time to decide—"Let me get back to you"—is one of the most underused and powerful tools you have.**

- When you break your own boundary, you repair it. No shame spiral required.

- Your voice belongs in the room. Use it before the resentment of not using it starts to cost you.

You have the words now. You know what to say, and you've practiced for tough situations. But knowing what to say and actually holding your boundary when someone reacts are two different skills.

Pushback, guilt, silence, and resistance don't mean your boundary failed. They just mean things are changing, and that change will feel uncomfortable for everyone, including you. That's normal. Remember, **it's okay to disappoint someone to protect your well-being**. Holding firm isn't cruel—it's being clear. Clarity keeps you from slipping back into old patterns you've worked hard to break.

In the next chapter, we'll talk about what happens after the boundary. How to stay steady when the pressure spikes, how to handle the emotional aftermath without caving, and how to keep trusting yourself when every old pattern is telling you to go back to the way things were.

Finding your voice is just the beginning. Learning to hold onto it when someone pushes back is how you truly become yourself.

6

When the Pushback Arrives — And It Will

Pushback isn't a sign that you set the wrong boundary. It's a sign you finally set the right one.

What Nobody Tells You About the Moment After

Read this slowly and let it sink in:

A boundary is not a request for someone else to change.
It's a decision about what you will do when they don't.

Setting a boundary is one thing. Keeping it in place when someone reacts—whether they get irritated, go cold, cry, guilt-trip, push back, or just look at you like you've changed completely—is something else. This chapter is about that moment, the one that comes after you finally speak up and the world doesn't applaud.

Boundaries seem empowering in theory. In reality, they bring up emotions, touch on old wounds, and disrupt habits that formed around your availability. You said something clear and honest, and now someone is upset. You might feel the urge to take it back, soften your words, apologize, or explain yourself over and over until everyone feels okay again.

Don't.

Their reaction isn't proof you did something wrong. It just shows change is uncomfortable for everyone, especially those who benefited from how things were. **Boundaries don't create problems. They reveal what was already there.**

Why Pushback Happens (And Why It's Not About You)

When you shift a pattern you've held for years, people notice. The version of you they were used to—the one who always said yes, always showed up, always absorbed the overflow—isn't showing up the same way anymore. That can be disorienting, even for people who love you.

Most pushback isn't malicious. It's discomfort with change, dressed up in whatever emotional costume that particular person defaults to. Someone who relies on your availability will resist losing it. Someone who mistook your limitlessness for devotion will interpret a limit as withdrawal. Someone who's never seen you say no will treat the first one like a betrayal. None of that is your fault, and none of it means you were wrong.

Pushback isn't failure. It's a recalibration, the natural friction that happens when a relationship adjusts to something more honest.

The Four Most Common Pushback Styles—and How to Respond

Think of pushback like weather patterns. Predictable. Recognizable. Manageable with the right preparation. Most people don't cycle through random reactions; they have a go-to style. Once you recognize it, you can respond to the pattern instead of getting swept up in the moment.

The Guilt-Tripper

The guilt-tripper uses your shared history as leverage. They bring up sacrifice, obligation, and memories to make you feel like your boundary is a debt you refuse to pay. Their goal, whether they realize it or not, is to make holding your limit feel harder than abandoning it.

You might hear: *"After everything I've done for you." "I guess I'm not important anymore." "You used to care."*

Your response stays warm and doesn't move:

- *"I care about you, and my decision stands."*

- *"I know this is disappointing. I'm still not able to do that."*

You don't need to defend your care record. **Your history together is not a payment plan for unlimited access.**

The Interrogator

The interrogator floods you with questions—not because they genuinely want to understand, but to wear you down. They hope that if they ask why enough times in different ways, you'll eventually give an answer they can challenge. As soon as you start justifying, they feel like they've won.

You might hear: *"Why?" "What changed?" "What's the real reason?" "Why can't you just...?"*

Your response keeps the focus on the decision, not the reasoning:

- *"There's nothing wrong. I'm just not available for this."*

- *"My decision is about my capacity, not about you."*

Their "confusion" doesn't obligate you to give a TED Talk.

The Minimizer

The minimizer tries to make your boundary seem like an overreaction so they can dismiss it. If they convince you that your needs don't matter, they don't have to change. Often, this comes from people who think being 'reasonable' just means agreeing with them.

You might hear: *"It's not that serious." "You're being dramatic." "You're making this weird."*

Your response stands firm without arguing about whether your boundary is valid:

- *"It might not feel big to you, but it matters to me."*

- *"This is still my boundary, regardless of how it lands for you."*

Your boundaries are valid, no matter others' responses. You don't need to prove it's a big deal. You just need to keep your boundary.

The Silent Punisher

The silent punisher doesn't argue; they pull away. You might notice cold energy, short replies, unread messages, or an obvious absence. The message is clear even without words: you did something wrong, and now you're going to feel it. This approach is meant to make your discomfort with the silence stronger than your commitment to your boundary, banking on you rushing to ease the tension.

You might notice: gone quiet, one-word responses, a coldness that wasn't there before, conspicuous absence from spaces where they used to show up.

Your response acknowledges the tension without surrendering to it:

- *"I can tell there's tension between us. I'm open to talking when you're ready, and my boundary stays the same."*

Silence doesn't require surrender. Their reaction is not an emergency that should take precedence over your well-being.

The Internal Battle: When the Loudest Pushback Is Your Own

Here's what nobody fully prepares you for: sometimes the other person handles your boundary completely fine, and you still feel like you did something unforgivable.

You said the thing. They heard it. Maybe they even respected it. And now you're lying awake at 11pm mentally rehearsing whether you were too harsh, whether you could have said it differently, whether you should just text and walk it back, whether the look on their face meant you permanently damaged something that mattered to you. You did the right thing, and it still feels like a wound.

That's post-boundary guilt, and it's different from pre-boundary anxiety. Pre-boundary anxiety is the fear of what might happen. Post-boundary guilt is your brain trying to convince you that what already happened was wrong, even when it wasn't.

That guilt isn't actually about this situation. It's about every time you held a similar line, and something went sideways. Every time you said no, someone left. Every time a need of yours caused conflict, and you learned early, in ways that went deep and stuck, that your needs weren't worth the disruption. That old wiring shows up now, right after you do the brave thing, dressed up as wisdom when it's really just a very old, very loud reflex.

That's when guilt feels most convincing, but that's also when it deserves the least influence over your next steps. When it spikes, try saying these things in your actual voice, not a scripted meditation app voice:

- *"I broke a pattern. Discomfort is what that feels like. It's not a signal to stop."*

- *"Someone being upset with me is not proof I was wrong."*

- ***"I can feel guilty and still be right."***

Let these reminders anchor you long enough for the initial wave to pass. Temporary discomfort follows boundaries, but it always fades.

When Boundaries Trigger Emotional Chaos

Most pushback fits into one of the four styles above. They're uncomfortable, but usually manageable and often improve over time. Some reactions, however, are much more intense, and it's important to recognize them if they happen to you.

Emotional chaos in response to a boundary can show up as an extreme reaction, like crying, rage, or threats, that doesn't match what you actually said. It might involve bringing in friends or family to argue their side, turning a private conversation into a group debate about your choices. Sometimes, they use your empathy against you, shifting quickly from your boundary to their crisis, making you feel like you caused an emergency just by stating a need. The conversation might suddenly include every complaint they've ever had, until you're defending your whole self instead of just one limit.

None of this means your boundary was wrong. It just means this person doesn't like being told no. That's their work to do, not yours.

Your job in those moments is not to de-escalate by abandoning yourself. You can acknowledge what someone is feeling without accepting responsibility for managing it: *"I understand you're upset. I'm still choosing what's best for me."*

Validation is not surrender. You can acknowledge someone's feelings and still keep your boundary. These two things can happen together, even if someone tries to make you think otherwise. Persistent escalation may signal deeper issues beyond the boundary itself.

Holding the Line Without Talking Yourself Out of It

Boundaries usually fall apart not because someone else overpowers you, but because you talk yourself out of them. You start explaining, adding context, offering alternatives, hedging, or apologizing. Somewhere in all that talking, the boundary quietly disappears, and you might not even notice when it happened.

The real power is in pausing and keeping things brief. You can take time before responding, even with people you care about. You can say less than you think you need to. A boundary doesn't become more valid the more you explain it; it just becomes easier to negotiate away. Short firm responses protect your boundaries best.

When you feel the urge to over-explain, reach for short instead:

- *"That doesn't work for me."*

- *"I'm not able to do that."*

- *"I hear you. My answer is still no."*

- *"I need space right now."*

- *"Let's revisit this another time."*

You don't owe anyone a conversation about a limit you've already made clear. These phrases work because they're complete. There's nothing to grab onto, nothing to argue with, no opening for the interrogator to pick apart. The discomfort you feel in the silence after saying one of these is not a sign you need to say more. Let the silence do its job.

When Breaking Your Own Boundary Is the Real Problem

Sometimes the person who needs the most from Chapter 5's repair scripts isn't someone else—it's you. You said yes when you meant no. You stayed longer, gave more, absorbed something you'd sworn you wouldn't absorb again.

It's important to notice how it feels when you break your own boundary after someone pushes back. That feeling can be especially discouraging. You held firm, someone pushed, and eventually you gave in. Now you might feel even worse than if you hadn't said anything in the first place.

That's not a reason to stop setting limits. It shows you which pressures are hardest for you to resist and which pushback styles affect you most. Pay attention to this. The mistake matters less than what it teaches you about where you need more support next time. Repair the situation using the language from Chapter 5, then keep moving forward.

When It's Time to Create Distance

Not every relationship survives your growth. Some people were comfortable when you ignored your own needs, and when you stop doing that, they feel abandoned—even though all you've done is create balance. The closeness they felt was built on your compliance. When that ends, it's not you changing; it's the relationship changing, because it was never as equal as it seemed.

That's a disorienting thing to realize about something you've been in for years. That realization deserves space before it requires a decision.

If someone keeps ignoring your limits after you've clearly stated them, uses silence or withdrawal to punish you for holding a boundary, treats your need for space as a personal attack, refuses to adjust no matter how you bring it up, or makes every conversation about their reaction to you, that pattern is telling you something. It's not about whether your boundary was wrong, but about what this relationship is really based on.

Distance is sometimes temporary, a period of less contact while things adjust. It can also last longer, or even be permanent, depending on what the relationship shows once you stop complying. What matters most is that you make the decision clearly and intentionally, not out of exhaustion or guilt. You're allowed to choose yourself, without making a big announcement or explaining yourself to people who have already shown they won't listen.

A quiet exit is still a valid exit.

Reflection: Your Pushback Map

Think about a specific situation where your boundary got pushback. Maybe someone reacted in a way that made you want to fold, explain yourself over and over, or take the whole thing back.

Ask yourself:

- Which of the four pushback styles were they using?

- What emotion rose in you when they reacted—guilt, fear, anger, the desperate need to fix it?

- What did you do with that emotion, and are you glad you did?

- If you could go back to that moment with everything you know now, what would you do differently—not perfectly, just differently?

- What's one sentence you'll use the next time that specific person pushes back in that specific way?

Write it down. Say it out loud. Your body will tell you if it feels true. The slight steadiness in your chest when you find the right words is real and worth noticing. The more you practice before the pressure comes, the less likely you'll need to recover from it later.

Small preparations lead to major relief.

Reminders

- **A boundary is not a request for someone else to change. It's a decision about what you will do when they don't.**

- The four pushback styles are predictable. When you recognize the pattern, you can respond to it instead of just reacting.

- Post-boundary guilt is different from pre-boundary anxiety. It's your old wiring trying to veto a decision you already made correctly.

- Post-boundary guilt is different from pre-boundary anxiety. It's your old wiring trying to veto a decision you already made correctly.

- Guilt isn't evidence that you were wrong. Someone being upset with you isn't either.

- Emotional chaos in response to a boundary is information about the relationship, not about the boundary.

- Holding your boundary means saying less, not more. Being brief helps you avoid talking yourself out of your own limit.

- Some people were comfortable with the version of you who had no limits. When you set boundaries, the relationship changes. That's not your failure; it's the relationship becoming more honest.

- A quiet exit is a valid exit.

When boundaries are new, pushback feels personal, like proof that you pushed too hard, asked for too much, or made a mistake. But as you keep holding them, something changes. Pushback starts to feel less like a judgment and more like information. It becomes less of a verdict and more of a guide to where you still need to work.

Eventually, something interesting happens: boundaries stop feeling like a reaction to other people's behavior and start feeling like an expression of who you are.

That's what the next chapter is about—not what boundaries protect you from, but what they make possible. Honoring your limits helps rebuild what compliance slowly wore away: your sense of worth, your trust in yourself, and your right to take up the space you deserve.

Boundaries don't just protect your peace. They shape the person you're becoming.

7

When Your Body Panics at Boundaries

You don't rediscover yourself by giving more. You rediscover yourself by releasing what was never yours to carry.

Your Body Has Been Running the Show: Here's the Map

All the tools in this book are already in your mind. The frameworks, scripts, and pushback strategies exist there, at least in theory. The challenge is that your body doesn't care about theory.

Here's the moment that exposes the gap: someone says, *"Can we talk?"* and your stomach drops. Your boss sends *"Quick question,"* and your heart rate spikes before you've even read the message. A friend asks for a favor, and your mouth says yes while your brain is still trying to form a sentence.

That's not a failure to understand. That's your body, and it has its own operating system that's been running much longer than any framework you've learned here. Until your body feels safe enough to set a limit, your mind's best intentions will keep getting pushed aside at the worst times.

This chapter focuses on your body's operating system: what it is, why it shapes your responses, and how to effectively work in alignment with it.

Fight, Flight, Freeze, Fawn: Your Body's Boundary Blueprint

These four responses aren't quirks. They are biological survival strategies, automatic and involuntary, shaped long before you had any concept of boundaries. They developed because, at some point, they worked for you. If they no longer help, it doesn't mean they're broken. It just means they need updating.

Fight: "I need to defend myself right now."

Your jaw tightens. Your tone sharpens without you meaning it to. A simple request you'd handle calmly on a good day suddenly feels like a threat, and your body reacts as if something critical is at stake—because in your body's memory, something once was. So you snap, get defensive, or interrupt the other person before they finish talking.

Fight responses show up when your internal alarm signals that you need to protect yourself fast. Anger becomes a shield. Control feels safer than vulnerability. You're not trying to create conflict; your body is trying to keep you from feeling powerless, and to your nervous system, conflict feels safer than helplessness.

Later, when the adrenaline fades, you might wonder why you reacted so strongly to something that, looking back, wasn't that serious. That confusion is the gap between your body's quick response and your brain's reasoning catching up. It doesn't mean you're volatile or unreasonable. It just means your alarm system fired before you could decide if the situation really called for it.

Flight: "I need to get out of here."

You avoid. You cancel. You suddenly remember something urgent that needs your attention somewhere else. You put off the conversation, distract yourself with your phone, or get busy with tasks you've ignored for weeks. Distance feels like relief, and right now, relief is all your body wants.

Flight is driven by fear that staying in a tough situation will make things worse—like criticism, emotional chaos, or conflict you can't win. If your past taught you that, your brain learned to leave before things get worse. But as you probably know, the conversation still waits. The boundary still needs to be set. The anxiety just changes shape, lingering in your mind until the next time, and the cycle repeats. Flight gives you short-term relief but no true resolution, which is why it never really works, no matter how often you try it.

Freeze: *"My mind just went completely blank."*

You open your mouth, and nothing comes out. You nod, even though you don't mean yes. Hours later—in the shower, driving home—the words you needed arrive with painful clarity. In the moment, everything locked: your thoughts, your voice, your ability to access anything you knew to be true.

Freeze happens when your internal alarm is so overwhelmed that shutting down seems like the only option. It's not weakness or stupidity. It's your body conserving resources when fight or flight aren't possible. This response was once protective, maybe when staying quiet kept you safer than speaking up. That wiring doesn't disappear just because the danger does. You can understand boundaries for years and still freeze under pressure. Knowing and acting aren't the same. The replay that happens afterward—*wondering why you didn't say anything, even though you knew what you wanted to say*—doesn't mean you failed. It just means your body responded faster than your words could.

Fawn: *"If I make them happy, I'll be safe."*

You over-explain before anyone asks for an explanation. You agree before you've had a chance to check if you're even available. You help when you're running on empty because helping feels safer than the alternative. You change into whatever version of yourself the moment seems to need—agreeable, accommodating, easy—because something in your past taught you that being those things was the best way to stay safe.

Fawn is rooted in the belief that approval equals safety. If love, belonging, or stability were conditional on your behavior growing up—if keeping the peace was how you avoided something worse—your body internalized a rule: make them happy, and you'll be okay. That rule became automatic. And ingrained rules don't pause to check whether the current situation actually warrants them.

This is the biological basis of everything Chapter 1 described. The people-pleasing, the immediate yes, the quiet "I'm fine" when you weren't—none of that was a character flaw or a weakness. It was fawn running the show, doing exactly what it was designed to do. The problem isn't that fawn exists. The problem is that it's been running on a threat assessment that's years out of date, protecting you from dangers that no longer exist in the same way, at the expense of the life you're trying to build now.

This is the one to watch most carefully, because it appears to be kindness. It earns you compliments for being easy to be around. It's the one that smiles and says, "Of course," while something inside feels empty. You give more than you have. You carry responsibilities that were never yours. The resentment that builds underneath isn't about the people you help; it's about never putting yourself on your own damn list.

That's the cost nobody talks about openly, and it's the one you're finally starting to recognize. Understanding fawn doesn't mean blaming your past or excusing harmful behavior from others. It means finally seeing the mechanism that's been running your responses, so you can choose something different.

They weren't conscious choices. They were survival defaults. And survival defaults can be retrained.

Why Your Body Treats Boundaries Like Threats

Now that you can name your default response, it helps to understand the deeper reason these responses get triggered in the first place. It's not about weakness, and it's not random.

Your body doesn't distinguish between emotional discomfort and physical danger. It responds to perceived threat—and perception is shaped by memory, not logic.

If you learned early that love, approval, or safety depended on keeping others comfortable, your brain stored a simple rule: disappointing someone equals danger. So now, saying "I can't today" or "that doesn't work for me" can trigger the same alarm your body reserves for actual emergencies. The words are small. The alarm is not. And because the alarm fires before your rational mind can step in, it can feel genuinely impossible to hold a boundary—even when every part of you knows you should.

This is why boundaries can feel terrifying even when you know they're reasonable. Your body remembers what it cost you not to comply, and it's trying to protect you from paying that price again. The good news, and it really is hopeful, is that your body can learn a different story. Not overnight, and not through willpower alone, but through repeated experiences: times when you held a limit and nothing terrible happened, when you said no and the relationship survived, and when protecting yourself turned out to be safe.

Every boundary you hold gives your body a new data point. Enough data points, and the threat assessment starts to update.

Regulation Tools: Practical Ways to Work With Your Body

Understanding why your body responds the way it does is the first step. The second is having something practical to use in the moment when your alarm goes off and you need to calm down enough to choose your response. These aren't wellness trends or feel-good affirmations; they are specific tools that calm your body's alarm system quickly enough to give your brain a chance to catch up. They're not about suppressing what you feel. They're about creating just enough space for your thinking brain to come back online before your default response takes over. When that happens, you can respond instead of react, and that's where your real choices begin.

The 4-6 Breath Reset

Inhale for four counts. Exhale for six. The longer exhale is the key because it signals to your body that the threat has passed, even before your mind has consciously registered safety. It slows your heart rate, releases tension in your chest and shoulders, and creates just enough calm for clearer thinking to return.

You can do this anywhere: in a meeting, in your car before a hard conversation, or while reading a text that made your stomach clench. It takes twelve seconds. No one will notice, but your body will. Think of it as hitting a brief pause on your internal alarm. You're not silencing it, just giving yourself enough room to think before you respond.

Name It to Tame It

Once you've taken a breath, the next step is to interrupt the spiral by naming what's actually happening. Say out loud if you can, or silently if not: "This *is anxiety, not danger. My body is reacting to something old. I'm allowed to pause.*"

Naming what's happening shifts your brain from running the emergency protocol to observing with a little more distance. **You're not denying the feeling. You're putting it in context.** The moment you name it, you create a small separation between you and your default response, which is enough to change what happens next. Over time, this practice trains your brain to stop treating every spike of discomfort as a five-alarm situation.

The 3-Point Grounding Check

When breathing and naming aren't enough, and your mind is still jumping between worst-case scenarios and old memories, bring it back to the present with something concrete. Notice one thing you can feel physically, like your feet on the floor, the chair under you, or the temperature of the air. Notice one thing you can see, such as the color of the wall, something on your desk, or what's outside the window. Notice one thing you can hear, like traffic, a fan, or someone's voice down the hall.

Three observations. That's it. What makes this work isn't the complexity; it's the redirection. Your body can't be fully activated and fully present at the same time. Grounding uses presence to interrupt the alarm by drawing your attention into the real moment instead of the feared one.

The Buffer Strategy

Sometimes the most important thing you can do is simply avoid responding right away. A buffer creates space between someone's request and your response, and that's exactly where your real choice lives. Without a buffer, you're responding from habit, from guilt, or from whatever your body's instinctive setting is in that moment.

"Let me check my schedule and get back to you." "I need a moment to think about that." "I'll follow up tomorrow." These aren't avoidance. They're like not sending an email when you're angry; they give your body time to settle before you commit to something your brain will regret. Most people agree to things they don't want to do simply because they responded before checking in with themselves first. The buffer helps prevent that.

The Bare Minimum Yes

If your body still isn't ready for a clean no—if even with breathing, grounding, and a buffer, the anxiety of a full refusal feels like too much right now—offer the smallest possible version of yes instead. *"I can help for ten minutes, but then I need to step away." "I can do one thing on this list, not all of them." "I can be there for part of it, not the whole thing."*

This isn't a compromise of your values. It's a bridge between the reflexive full compliance your body has learned and the full self-advocacy you're working toward. You're practicing limits in doses your body can handle, because that's how new patterns get established. Not through dramatic overnight change, but through incremental evidence that show the world doesn't collapse when you offer a smaller yes, and nothing terrible happens when you hold even a partial limit.

Progress doesn't require perfection. It requires practice.

How Your History Shaped Your Body's Responses

The tools above are practical—you can use them starting today. But understanding why your body defaults to fight, flight, freeze, or fawn in the first place can make a significant difference in how compassionately you respond to yourself when those defaults show up. Because they will show up. And knowing where they came from makes it easier to work with them instead of against yourself.

Your alarm system wasn't formed in isolation. It developed inside particular environments with specific people under distinct kinds of pressure—and it remembers all of it, even when you don't consciously.

If you grew up in a culture where saying no was framed as disrespect, or in a family where love felt conditional on your behavior, or in a household where emotional unpredictability meant you needed to stay constantly alert, your body learned to scan for threat before it ever learned to rest. If your primary strategy for staying safe was keeping people happy, your body got very efficient at fawning. If speaking up reliably led to conflict or punishment, freeze or flight became your defaults. Those responses weren't random. They were the smartest available option given what you were working with at the time.

Past relationships add to this. If you've been in situations where manipulation, control, or emotional volatility were common, your body may still be tuned to that environment. This means situations that are genuinely safe today can still trigger old responses. A partner asking a reasonable question might feel like an interrogation. A friend expressing disappointment might seem like the start of something much worse. Your body isn't stuck in the past on purpose. It's doing what it learned to do when that past was happening, and updating that learning takes gradual, intentional work. That's exactly what you're doing by reading this book and using these tools.

None of this excuses others' behavior, and none of it means you're trapped. It's context, and context turns confusion into clarity. When you understand why your body responds the way it does, you stop fighting yourself for having the response and start working with it instead. That shift alone can change things more than you might expect.

If you're carrying the added weight of a marginalized identity, high-responsibility roles, or the pressure to represent your community, your body has been doing extra work for a long time, often without acknowledgment or rest. The fear of being labeled difficult, ungrateful, or too much is real, and it shapes your responses in specific ways that aren't always visible to people who haven't lived them.

Exhaustion is not a requirement for belonging. Choosing yourself is not the same as abandoning the people you love.

Reflection: Reading Your Own Body

Think of a recent moment when your body reacted before your words did, such as when you agreed too soon, went quiet, snapped at someone, or suddenly needed to be somewhere else.

Ask yourself:

- Which of the four responses showed up—fight, flight, freeze, or fawn?

- What triggered the reaction?

- What tool could help next time?

- What sentence can anchor me when pressure rises?

Write your answers down. Progress isn't measured by never reacting. It's measured by how quickly you return to yourself after your body responds. Your nervous system is relearning safety, slowly and gently. The more you understand your own patterns, the faster that return becomes.

Your body has been telling you the truth for years. This is where you start listening.

Reminders

- **Your history explains your responses. It doesn't sentence you to them.**

- Boundaries are biological events, not just mental decisions. Your body has its own response system, and it has been running longer than any framework you've learned.

- Fight, flight, freeze, and fawn are survival strategies, not character flaws. They were shaped by experience, not chosen.

- Fawn is the biological root of people-pleasing, automatic compliance, and the gradual loss of self that comes from making approval your main safety strategy.

- **Your body treats boundaries like threats because it learned at some point that disappointing people was dangerous. That programming can be updated through repetition and safe experiences.**

- The regulation tools—breathing, naming, grounding, buffering, and the bare minimum yes—work in sequence. Each one builds on the last and gives your thinking brain a little more room to catch up with your body's alarm. **Exhaustion is not a requirement for belonging. Choosing yourself is not the same as abandoning the people you love.**

When your body starts to feel safer holding a limit, something changes. The boundary stops feeling like something you have to brace for and struggle through, and starts feeling like just the way you move through the world.

That's the shift: from 'I'm trying to have boundaries' to 'I'm someone who has them.' Chapter 8 explores what that identity shift looks like in daily life.

The work you've done in this book isn't just changing your behavior. It's changing who you believe you are.

8

Holding Your Ground When Life Gets Loud

The goal isn't perfect boundaries. The goal is a life that feels like yours again.

This Is What Maintenance Actually Looks Like

Growth doesn't happen in dramatic breakthroughs. It happens on the ordinary days when life is loud, you're tired, and everything is quietly lobbying for you to go back to the way things were.

Your calendar explodes. Your family needs something. Work doubles down on the urgency. A friendship gets complicated. Your sleep goes sideways, and your patience goes with it. The version of you who had all these tools and all this clarity starts to feel like someone you were briefly acquainted with last month.

That's maintenance mode, and it's the real test of everything this book has built. Because anyone can hold a limit when they're rested and clear-headed, and the stakes feel manageable. The question is what happens when life gets loud, when old dynamics resurface, when the people around you start pushing to see if the change sticks.

Boundaries aren't something you achieve once. They're something you practice—like strength training for self-respect. The real work isn't the first time you show up. It's the Tuesday when you don't feel like it, when nothing is dramatic or urgent, when you could easily skip it and tell yourself you'll do better next week.

This chapter is about that Tuesday.

The Daily Check-In — Know Where You Stand Before the Day Starts Pulling

Boundaries weaken fastest when you lose track of yourself—not all at once, but in the small, gradual drift that happens when your attention goes entirely outward and nobody's checking on what's happening inside.

Before the day claims you, take sixty seconds and ask yourself three things:

- *How much capacity do I have today—honestly?* Not how much you think you should have, not the amount that would let you avoid disappointing anyone, but what's genuinely available.

- *Where is the pressure most likely to show up?* You know your life. You know which conversations, which people, which situations are likely to test you today. Name them before they arrive.

- *What is the one thing I need to protect most?* Not a comprehensive list. One thing—your energy, your time, a conversation you're not ready to have, a commitment you need to keep with yourself.

That's it. Three questions, sixty seconds, done before anyone else has a vote on how your day goes. When you check in with yourself first, you make decisions from awareness rather than from urgency. You respond from choice instead of habit. Those sixty seconds are the difference between responding to your life and just reacting to it.

Write It Down. Your Growth Deserves a Witness.

Here's something that happens to almost everyone doing this work: you forget how far you've come. It's not because you're not paying attention, but because progress here is quiet. It doesn't announce itself. There's no moment when someone gives you a certificate that says "Congratulations, you have officially stopped abandoning yourself." The wins are small and ordinary, like the request you didn't immediately say yes to, the conversation you redirected, or the plan you canceled without a long apology.

And then you have a hard week, and your inner critic shows up with a list of everything you've done wrong lately, and suddenly it feels like you haven't made any progress at all.

Writing it down is how you fight that lie.

You don't have to journal beautifully or every day. Even a few sentences, a few times a week, specifically tracking your boundary moments—when you held one, when you slipped, when you felt the pull and chose differently—creates something your memory alone can't: a record. Actual evidence that change is happening, in your own words, from your own experience, that your inner critic can't easily dismiss because you wrote it yourself.

The most useful thing to notice isn't just the wins. It's the patterns. Which situations keep coming up? Which people show up most often in the tough moments? Where do you tend to lose your footing, and what's usually happening when that occurs? Patterns give you information. They show you where your limits need more support, where you're getting stronger, and where you still have work to do. That's the evidence you need when doubt appears and tries to convince you nothing has changed. And it will show up. Write it down anyway.

Find Your "Nope, That's the Old You" Person

Change is easier when someone else can see it happening. Their role isn't to police your choices, but to remind you of your intentions on days when you forget why you're doing this.

The right accountability partner for this work is someone who understood the old dynamic, who saw you over-give, over-explain, and over-extend, and who truly cares about the version of you that doesn't do that anymore. Not someone who will judge you when you slip, but someone who will look at you when your mind starts to negotiate—maybe I'm overreacting, maybe it's not that serious, maybe I should just say yes—and say, without apology: "Nope. That's the old you talking."

That level of detail matters. Accountability for boundary work isn't just generic life coaching. It takes someone who understands what you're trying to change, what your patterns look like, and what your inner voice sounds like when you're about to give in.

It's someone who can spot "you're rationalizing again" even when you make it sound reasonable.

If you don't have that person yet, structure can help in the same way. A weekly self-check, even just five minutes asking yourself:

- Did I honor my limits this week?

- Where did I wobble?

- What do I need more of going forward?

These questions help you stay honest with *yourself*. The goal is to see yourself clearly enough to make changes before a small slip turns into a bigger setback.

Slipping Doesn't Mean Starting Over. It Means You're Still in the Game.

The earlier chapters covered the first-time slip. This one is about the fifth time. The one that happens four months in, when you thought you had this handled, when you'd been doing so well, and then someone hit exactly the right button, and you folded instantly, as if none of it had happened.

That particular discouragement—"I thought I was past this"—is one of the most defeating feelings in this whole process. And it will happen. Not because you weren't making real progress, but because the pressures that created your patterns in the first place don't disappear just because you've been working on yourself. They resurface. Especially when you're tired, or sick, or stressed, or when the person pushing is someone who knew you before and still has all the leverage that history provides.

When it happens, don't let yourself spiral. Instead, notice it without making it into something bigger than it is. One slip after months of growth doesn't mean you haven't changed. It shows that change takes time, old patterns run deep, and you're playing by different rules now than you were a year ago. So when you slip, you're slipping from a higher starting point than before.

You don't have to pretend the slip didn't happen. You acknowledge it, you figure out what triggered it—not to punish yourself, but because the trigger is useful information about where your limits still need reinforcement—and you course-correct. Quietly, directly, without turning it into a referendum on whether you're capable of change. Just like muscles shake when they're getting stronger, boundaries can feel shaky while they're forming. The shaking is not the problem. Stopping is.

Setbacks are detours, not dead ends. You grow by returning to yourself faster each time—and eventually, the return trip gets shorter.

When Life Finally Reflects Who You've Become

The self-help version of thriving with boundaries involves a list of changes—less anxiety, clearer decisions, stronger self-trust—that sounds good but means very little until you're living it. So let's be specific about what it feels like for the woman this book was written for.

It's the Sunday that doesn't come with dread anymore. Not because your week got easier, but because you stopped filling it with obligations you'd already half-agreed to and were quietly resenting all week. It's waking up on Monday and knowing that what's on your calendar is there because you intentionally put it there, not because you couldn't figure out how to say no in time.

It's a text from someone asking for something, and your first feeling isn't panic—it's just consideration. Do I want to? Do I have the capacity? Those questions arise naturally now, before the automatic yes has a chance to fire. That's new. You didn't have that before.

It's the conversation you redirected before it became the hour-long emotional download you used to absorb in silence and resent later. It's the favor you declined without a three-paragraph explanation, and finding out—again, surprisingly—that the friendship survived. It's the meeting you left on time. The call you didn't pick up because you were in the middle of something that mattered to you.

It's saying yes and meaning it—freely, without the undercurrent of obligation—because yes now means something different than it used to. **When you stopped saying yes to everything, your yeses became real.** People can feel the difference, even if they can't name it.

It's not that your life got simpler. It's that your participation in it got more intentional. You stopped managing everyone else's comfort and started managing your own presence. That shift is quieter than you expected. Less dramatic. But it shows up in the quality of an ordinary Tuesday in a way that no single boundary conversation ever could.

Boundaries don't shrink your life. They create the space for the life you actually want.

Reflection: Your Maintenance Audit

Think about the last two or three weeks—not the dramatic moments, but the everyday ones. Where did you hold your ground without making it a whole thing? Where did you feel the familiar pull toward the old pattern and choose differently, even if only slightly? Where did you slip, and what was going on when it happened?

Ask yourself:

- What triggered me recently—and what emotion surfaced first?

- What did I need in that moment that I didn't give myself?

- What boundary would have protected me?

- What does my life look like right now when it's working—what's present that wasn't before?

- What still needs the most attention?

- What's one thing I could do this week to stay connected to the work, even if life is loud?

Write it all down. Not as a performance of progress, but as an honest check-in with yourself. Your answers become a roadmap—not just for what to fix, but for how far you've already come.

Reminders

- **Maintenance is the real work. Anyone can hold a limit when conditions are ideal. The growth is in what you do on the ordinary, difficult Tuesday.**

- A 60-second daily check-in keeps you responding from choice instead of habit.

- Writing down your boundary moments creates the evidence your inner critic can't argue with and the patterns your intuition needs to see.

- Accountability—through people or reflection—keeps you aligned when doubt and old patterns return.

- **Mistakes provide guidance for improvement.** The fifth slip after months of growth is not proof that you haven't changed. It's proof that change is a long game, and you're still in it.

- Thriving doesn't look like a sudden transformation. It looks like the Sunday that doesn't come with dread, the text you considered before responding, the yes that finally means something because it's a real one.

- **Growth happens through repetition and reflection.** Boundaries don't shrink your life. They create the space for the life you want.

All of this—the check-ins, the journaling, the setbacks, the daily maintenance—is the work of becoming someone. Not just someone who has better habits, but someone whose relationship to herself has fundamentally shifted. Someone who takes up the space she's entitled to, not because she's worked herself into it, but because she's finally stopped talking herself out of it.

That's what Chapter 9 is about. Not the techniques or the scripts, but the woman who has internalized all of it—how she moves through the world, how she makes decisions, and how the quiet accumulation of holding her own limits has rebuilt something in her that compliance quietly eroded for years.

This is where the work becomes who you are. And where the woman you've been building toward finally takes the lead.

9

Who You Become When You Stop Shrinking

When you stop shrinking for others, you finally meet the version of yourself you were always meant to become.

The Question Nobody Prepares You For

Everyone shows you how to say no, spot guilt-trips, and stand your ground when others push back. But almost no one talks about what happens next, when everything gets quiet and calm, and you find yourself in a stillness that feels strange because you've never been there before. In that quiet, a question can show up that feels even more confusing than any boundary talk you've had:

Who the hell am I without all the over-giving?

For years, maybe even decades, your identity might have centered on being the helper. The dependable one. The person who picks up the slack, takes on extra burdens, and manages everyone's emotions. These roles weren't just personality traits—they were ways to cope. They kept relationships going, made others comfortable, and helped you stay safe in places where your value depended on being useful.

When you stop taking on those roles, everything gets quieter. There's no crisis to handle on a Saturday morning, no emotional emergency to fix, and no request to agree to before you've had a chance to think. In that quiet, you might not feel relief right away. Instead, it can feel like vertigo, as if the floor shifted and you haven't found your footing yet.

That's the identity vacuum. And it's exactly where the real work begins.

Here's what no one fucking tells you: peace can feel strange at first. If your body has been wired to live with urgency and tension, calm might seem unfamiliar or even unsettling. Your body might interpret the quiet as something risky rather than safe. That reaction doesn't mean you're doing something wrong. It just means you're learning a new way to live after years of surviving on adrenaline.

The space that's opening up used to be filled with obligations, performances, and roles you never really chose. Now it belongs to you, but it doesn't feel familiar yet because you've never lived in it before. You might feel sad about letting go of the part of yourself that kept everything together. That sadness is real and deserves attention. But it doesn't mean something went wrong. It means something old is ending, and something new that truly belongs to you is starting.

When that happens, the metric changes. You stop proving your worth by wearing yourself out. Instead, you build it by making choices that align with who you are, one step at a time.

The Old You Got You Here. She Can't Take You Further.

No one tells you that when you start setting boundaries, your old life won't fit anymore. The version of you who kept everything running—the fixer, the peacemaker, the emotional sponge, the friend who always listened—starts to feel unfamiliar. You begin to outgrow roles you spent your whole damn life learning.

The issue isn't that you created these roles. It's that they became habits, and habits don't always check if the situation still warrants them.

When you stop taking on those roles, things change in a way that can feel confusing. The urgency fades. The pressure eases. You wake up on a quiet Saturday morning with no crisis to handle, no fires to put out, and no emotional mess to clean up. You look around and wonder: *Now that I'm not needed, who am I?*

That feeling isn't emptiness. It's freedom in its purest, unfamiliar form, and your body doesn't trust it yet because you've never experienced it before.

Unlearning old patterns feels awkward, almost like using your non-dominant hand. Your brain and body created real pathways around those behaviors. Choosing a new response takes effort, practice, and patience with feeling clumsy in situations where you used to feel comfortable. That clumsiness isn't failure. It's your brain making new paths while the old ones are still there, still tempting you to return to what's familiar.

What helps during this time isn't more information or motivation. It's being curious in a specific way. Instead of asking, "what's *wrong with me?*" try asking, *"what did I give away that I want back?"* Instead of *"why can't I just get this right?"* ask, *"what was true about me before I started performing?"*

The answers won't arrive as sudden revelations. They show up without announcement—in the thing you reach for when no one is watching, the company that doesn't leave you drained, the activity you keep almost doing and then talking yourself out of. Pay attention to those moments. Write them down. They're the outline of the person you truly are, starting to come into focus.

You aren't losing yourself in this process. You're letting go of the survival identity you created to stay connected no matter what. The discomfort shows that something old is ending.

To create a new self, you need to let go of the version of you shaped by survival.

What Self-Worth Actually Looks Like in Real Life

People often think self-worth is just a feeling, something inspirational or abstract. But in reality, self-worth is very practical. It appears in daily choices, especially the small ones no one else notices.

Self-worth means saying no to invitations when you're tired, protecting your time without giving long explanations. It means trusting your own judgment instead of seeking reassurance from others. It means resting without feeling you have to justify it.

You don't chase people who choose confusion. You don't bargain for love. You don't tolerate emotional crumbs. You don't abandon yourself to keep someone comfortable.

Self-worth isn't loud. It's steady. It's a quiet confidence that says:

If access to me requires self-abandonment, the answer is no.

That's not selfishness. That's finally standing up for yourself.

That's self-worth at the surface level. Here's what it looks like when it goes deeper.

Self-Worth Is a Presence, Not a Feeling

People often describe self-worth as an emotional state, something you feel on good days and lose on tough ones. While inner work matters, self-worth in daily life is much more practical and much less dramatic.

Self-worth appears as your default. It's in how you respond to an invitation when you're tired—you simply say no, without a long explanation or guilt. It's in the moment when someone tries the old tricks, like guilt-tripping or suggesting your limits are a betrayal, and you don't react the way you used to.

That last example is worth sitting with for a while. The change from being easily manipulated to standing firm isn't a one-time decision. It builds up over time. Each time you kept your boundary when someone pushed, let someone be disappointed without rushing to fix it, or felt guilty but acted anyway, you built something inside yourself—a kind of inner strength that makes old tactics land differently than they used to.

When your worth lives in your bones, manipulation finds nothing to grip. Guilt trips only work if you believe you owe something you don't. Emotional pressure only works if you care more about their comfort than your own integrity. These tactics only succeed when you're still using the old mindset—the one that made their approval your measure. When your measure changes, everything changes.

Clarity isn't cruelty. It's growth. The people who truly care about you—not just what you *do* for them—will meet you in that growth. Those who can't will show you, through their reactions, what the relationship was really based on. Don't avoid that information. It may not feel comfortable, but it's valuable.

This is rebuilding. This is reclaiming. This is you becoming someone who treats your needs as important—because they fucking are.

The Peace Era — Soft, Steady, and Unapologetic

Let's be honest about what peace truly looks like, because it is nothing like what anyone told you it would be.

It's not a spa weekend. It's not a break from your life. It's not a moment of perfect clarity where everything makes sense. Most of the time, peace is quiet and ordinary, and that ordinariness can feel strange after years of living with emotional intensity.

Your peace era won't look like a wellness influencer's reel. There won't be soft lighting or a piano soundtrack. No one is clapping because you went to bed early. No one is applauding the text you didn't answer until the next day, the plan you canceled because your body needed rest, the argument you walked away from because you realized you were being asked to perform in someone else's battlefield.

It might mean not explaining yourself to people who have already made up their minds. It might mean going home early and genuinely feeling glad about it. It could be sitting with a difficult feeling without rushing to fix it. It might mean letting a relationship be what it is, instead of trying to change it into what you want.

Peace isn't passive. It doesn't avoid confrontation out of fear. It chooses not to engage in certain conflicts because it can clearly see which ones were never really about you, and which ones were just opportunities for someone else to access what they used to get easily.

Boring isn't failure. Boring is stability. And stability is where healing finally sticks.

As time passes and you practice this consistently, something shifts. The craving for intensity—the drama, the urgency, the emotional peaks that used to pass for connection—starts to quiet down. What you want instead is different: consistency, predictability, relationships where you can finally relax. Environments where you're not scanning for what's about to go wrong. People around whom you can be a person, not just a function.

Some days, old urges will return—the panic, the impulse to over-give, the voice telling you to check in, fix things, and make sure everyone's okay. That doesn't mean you're slipping back. It just means the old patterns are still there, looking for a chance. You don't have to let them in.

Peace is a boundary, a decision, and a daily fucking practice. Each time you choose it instead of the familiar chaos, you teach yourself something important: you can be steady and whole without having to earn it through exhaustion.

This kind of peace isn't an affirmation to memorize. It's a standard to live by.

Reflection: Rewrite Your Self-Story

Take your time with these. Read each one and sit with it before moving to the next.

Ask yourself:

- Who were you when your limits were fragile—which roles were you performing, and for whom?

- What part of your old identity have you stopped performing, even imperfectly?

- What part of yourself are you no longer willing to negotiate away?

- What versions of you are you ready to release—not with bitterness, but with understanding?

- Who are you becoming as your limits get clearer and your voice gets steadier?

- What parts of yourself are you claiming now, without apology, that you spent years dimming?

- What feels more authentically yours today than it did a year ago?

Write your answers. Don't worry about making them perfect or fast—just be honest. Then write a single paragraph titled:

The Version of Me I'm Choosing Now

Write it as a promise to yourself. Write it sincerely. Make it specific to your real life—not just a general statement about self-worth, but about *you*. Include the things you're no longer willing to accept, what you're working toward, and the kind of woman you're becoming in the quiet, everyday moments no one else sees.

That paragraph is yours. It belongs to no one else. And it will mean more to you six months from now than any affirmation you could memorize today.

Take This With You

- **The identity vacuum isn't where you lose yourself. It's where you finally discover who you really are.**

- You weren't weak. You were strategic. That adaptation can be unlearned.

- When you stop using the old mindset, manipulation loses its grip—not because you became tougher, but because you became clearer.

- **Self-worth isn't a feeling you summon. It's a presence that accumulates through repeated choices to honor your own limits.**

- Clarity is not cruelty. It's growth.

- Peace is ordinary. Boring is stability. Stability is where healing finally sticks.

- *Remember this one: If access to you requires self-abandonment, the answer is no.*

By now, boundaries aren't just something you're learning. They're becoming part of who you are—in how you respond to requests, how you start and end conversations, and how you use your time, care, and presence.

The last chapter is about living from that place—not as a project you're always working on, but as the foundation of a life that finally feels like your own.

The destination was never just stronger boundaries. It was becoming someone you don't abandon to be loved.

10

The Woman on the Other Side

The moment you stop abandoning yourself, life stops handing you people who mirror your old wounds.

This Chapter Is About Her

*Y*ou made it.

You haven't reached the end of a book, but the start of something real. This chapter is about her, the woman who emerged after all your hard work. She's the one your past self hoped for during tough times. She isn't just a dream or a goal. She's the real you, waiting for you to stop holding yourself back.

Boundaries aren't the end goal. They're the entry point. On the other side is a life that truly belongs to you—not one shaped by your constant availability or by doing too much for others, but a life that starts when you stop questioning your worth and begin making choices based on it.

That's where we're going.

Peace Isn't a Treat — It's the Standard

It can take a long time to believe this: consistency isn't boring. Predictability doesn't mean there's no excitement. Being in a relationship where you aren't always on edge isn't settling. It's what you always deserved, even if you once thought it was too much to hope for.

The woman you're becoming understands this now. She doesn't just find peace on good days and chase it on the hard ones. She guards her peace as carefully as she once guarded other people's comfort, but now she focuses on herself. She does this with care and consistency, because it matters—and she's finished pretending it doesn't.

Her standards aren't too high—they're finally healthy. She doesn't keep explaining herself to people who don't listen. She no longer holds onto relationships that only work when they benefit someone else. She knows the difference between being close to someone and performing for them, between truly being present and just managing things, and between love that's given freely and love that requires constant effort.

When someone in her life gives less than she does, or when the effort is one-sided, and her needs are always set aside, she notices it calmly, without drama. She responds by quietly changing her own actions, letting herself know that she's not willing to keep doing this.

Peace isn't something she earned by wearing herself out. It's her starting point. It's where she always returns, and she won't leave for long.

There She Is

Picture her. Not perfectly. Just honestly.

Yes, she's a badass—but a peaceful one.

She moves differently now—slower and with more confidence. It's not because life became easier, but because she stopped dividing her attention between her own thoughts and what others want to hear. She makes decisions without needing approval first. She changes her mind without feeling the need to apologize for her past opinions.

She still loves deeply. That hasn't changed. But now she loves without desperation or trying to prove she's worth keeping. She gives generously, but not without limits. She forgives easily, but not over and over. She lets people in and allows them to show her who they are, believing them the first time instead of making excuses until it's impossible to ignore.

Her softness came back. It was always there, underneath the armor she needed during the years she was figuring this out. But now it has teeth.

Her heart is gentle, but her boundaries? Sharp as fuck.

She leaves early instead of waiting too long—whether it's from conversations that go nowhere, relationships that have become obligations, or places where she's expected but not valued. She doesn't wait until she feels empty to go. She leaves while she still has something left and doesn't spend weeks doubting her choice.

When someone uses old tactics like guilt, questioning, giving her the cold shoulder, or saying "I thought you cared about me," she doesn't react the way she once did. It's not because she's become cold or stopped caring. It's because she now knows that caring for someone and betraying herself to keep them comfortable are not the same, and she no longer mixes them up.

That woman isn't someone you're watching from afar anymore. She's you.

One day, you simply stop chasing—not out of anger, ego, or pride, but because you're clear. Once you've felt emotional safety, anything that doesn't fit feels uncomfortable. You stop looking for what might go wrong or adjusting yourself to others' moods. When something feels off, you just notice it instead of treating it like a crisis.

Your future self knows something your past self didn't: **if someone makes you doubt your worth, your sanity, or your reality, that isn't chemistry. That's conditioning.**

And she refuses to go back.

What You Get Back — And How the World Shifts

When you stop hemorrhaging energy to relationships that take more than they give, to obligations that were never yours, and to always managing others' emotions, something unexpected happens.

The creative spark you thought was gone returns—not all at once, but in small, steady ways. You become interested in things again, curious, and aware of your own preferences in a way that feels new, even though these parts of you were always there, waiting for things to quiet down.

You regain your focus. Decisions that once took days now come more quickly, because you're no longer worrying about how others will react. You trust your own judgment. You don't need as much reassurance before acting. You want to rest without feeling you have to justify it.

Clarity creates capacity. Boundaries create bandwidth. Healing creates momentum.

Your environment changes too—not because others suddenly changed, but because you did. The coworker who used to give you last-minute tasks might still try, but when you respond calmly, without apologizing or checking whether they're upset, they recalibrate. The friend who only called during her own emergencies might still reach out, but when you're sometimes unavailable or suggest something more balanced, the relationship either becomes more equal or shows it never was.

People don't suddenly mature. You just stop giving them permission to treat you the way they always did. Bullshit stops slipping through the cracks because you finally sealed your boundary leaks.

Reflection: A Letter From Future You

This is one of the most important reflections in the in the book.

Write a letter. Write it as her, the woman you're becoming. Let her speak to the version of you who is holding this book right now, in whatever moment you're in.

Let her tell you:

- What she's proud of you for—be specific, not general.

- What she's no longer putting up with, and how quietly and simply that happened.

- What she wants you to let go of—the role, the relationship, the story, or the version of yourself that put others' comfort before your own truth.

- What she wants you to fiercely protect—without apology, even if it costs you something.

- What she wants you to remember, especially on days when old habits return and the progress feels far away.

- What she wants you to stop apologizing for, starting now.

- What she knows you can do, even if you can't see it yet.

Write it in your own words. Not the polished version. The true one.

Seal it. Fold it. Keep it somewhere sacred.

Revisit it whenever you feel yourself slipping—not to shame yourself for the slip, but to remember who you are when you're at your best. Because growth isn't about never struggling again. It's about having something to return to when you do.

Take This With You

- You aren't just a dream to aspire to. You are the real thing, once you stop holding yourself back.

- Peace isn't something you earn by suffering. It's your standard. Protect it, because it matters.

- Your gentle side returned, but now it has teeth.

- You give generously, but not without limits. You forgive easily, but not repeatedly. Your heart is gentle, but your boundaries are strong as hell.

- Clarity creates capacity. Boundaries create bandwidth. Healing creates momentum.

- No one grows up for you. You simply stop accepting treatment that assumes you won't notice.

- Every time you chose yourself, even if it wasn't perfect or confident, even if no one noticed, you were building this. You were building her.

Future You isn't created by big speeches, perfect boundary talks, or one big moment of honesty. She's built through quietly and repeatedly refusing to abandon yourself—in the small moments no one sees, in the requests you pause before answering, in the obligations you turn down without a long apology, and in the times you feel guilty but still do what's right.

She's built on Tuesdays. In ordinary moments. In the accumulation of choosing yourself, again and again, until it stops feeling like a choice and starts feeling like just the way you move through the world.

You've been building her this whole time.

She's already here.

Welcome home.

11

Beyond Boundaries — The Life You're Building Now

A woman who knows her worth doesn't walk into a room looking for approval. She walks in knowing she belongs everywhere she decides to stand.

Beyond Boundaries: The Next Level Nobody Talks About

After you reclaim your peace, belonging stops being something you chase. It becomes something you assume.

That's the shift. Not learning boundaries or practicing them—but living like they're part of you. Boundaries are no longer something you reach for when things fall apart. They become the way you move through the world—steady, clear, and unapologetic. Not a rule. Not a reaction. A standard.

But here's the distinction most books never reach—and it's the one that changes everything:

A boundary draws a line. A standard defines who you are.

These two things work together, but they are not the same. A boundary is responsive. It shows up when something threatens your peace—when a request exceeds your capacity, when someone crosses a limit you've stated, when a situation asks more of you than you have to give. A boundary says *"this doesn't work for me."* It's specific. It's situational. And it requires energy every time you enforce it.

A standard is different. A standard is the decision you make before the situation arrives—the principle you've already settled on, not in response to someone crossing a line, but because you finally got clear on who you are and what belongs in your life. A standard says *"I don't allow this into my life anymore."* It doesn't react. It doesn't negotiate. It simply holds.

Here's the practical difference: a boundary requires you to be present, activated, and ready to enforce. A standard removes the need for that conversation in the first place. When your standards are clear, fewer things get close enough to require a boundary. The filter happens upstream—and that's where the real freedom lives.

What Standards Actually Look Like

Here's the clarity most people spend years trying to find, and few explain well: standards aren't just rules you write down and try to remember when things get tough. They're decisions you've made so clearly and completely that they work automatically, just like your best habits.

They sound like this in real life: if something keeps disrupting your peace, it loses access to you—not after another talk or another chance, but simply as a rule. If communication in a relationship causes more confusion than clarity, you step back without guilt or long explanations. If someone's effort is inconsistent, showing up only when they want something and disappearing when you need support, intimacy doesn't grow, because you've already decided that's not the kind of relationship you want. If respect is missing from an interaction, you quietly remove yourself. It's not dramatic. It's just who you are no w.

These aren't reactions to what someone did. They're decisions you made about what you allow, made ahead of time from a place of clarity, not crisis. That's why they hold up under pressure, even when boundaries sometimes don't. They don't break, chase approval, or ask for understanding. **Boundaries can be debated. Standards are simply how you**

live.

Standards become anchors. Over time, they make everything simpler. You spend less time debating with yourself—should I speak up, *should I let it go, am I overreacting*—because you've already answered those questions deep down. The negotiation is over. The decision is made. You just live by it. That's the real power of standards. They don't just protect your peace. They protect your future.

The question that keeps you grounded when old habits return is: *How would the healed version of me handle this?* Not the version who used to go along just to keep the peace, but the one who's grown beyond that. Act from her perspective, especially when your voice trembles, when guilt appears, and when the easy way out seems tempting.

Anyone Who Leaves When You Stop Complying Wasn't Staying for You

When your standards get clear, some relationships shift. Some people rise to meet you—they adjust without resentment, they respect the new dynamic, they're glad to know where you stand because it helps them show up more honestly too. Those relationships deepen. Keep them close.

Others drift away. It's not because you became difficult or changed too much. They leave because the version of you they depended on—the one who gave too much, explained too much, and stayed quiet to keep the peace—is gone. Without that compliance, the relationship no longer has a foundation they want to build on.

Your boundaries exposed their expectations. Your growth exposed their comfort with the old dynamic. Your self-respect exposed the imbalance. Let them go.

That's not a loss. That's clarity.

Anyone who leaves when you stop abandoning yourself was never really there for you. They were there for the version of you who didn't have boundaries yet. Now that you've reclaimed yourself, you can finally see the difference, and that's both disorienting and freeing in this whole process.

Let the disorientation exist. Let the grief be there if it needs to be. And let the clarity do its work.

She Tried. She Got You Here. She Can't Take You Further.

Here's what nobody says about the version of you that kept everything running: she tried. She coped. **She accepted crumbs because she had never been shown what a full meal looked like.** She apologized for having needs and mistook self-sacrifice for love.

She got you this far. But she can't take you where you're headed.

Reinvention isn't about becoming someone unrecognizable. It's about finally becoming undeniable. It's the steady result of small, consistent, and quietly brave choices that create a life that fits you, not just the version of you who learned to survive.

Vision — What You're Building Toward

Boundaries without direction can start to feel like a series of walls: things you keep out, limits you enforce, situations you avoid. Protection is important and real, but it's not the whole point.

The whole point is creation. You're not just building a defended life. You're building an *actual* life—one that reflects who you are, what you value, and what you want your days to feel like from the inside. The question shifts from what you're walking away from to what you're walking toward. That distinction matters more than it sounds.

That takes vision. Not just a mood board or a list of wishes and manifestations, but a clear and honest picture of what you're building. This way, your standards, limits, and choices all point toward something intentional, not just away from things you don't want.

Picture it specifically. What does your morning feel like when you wake up without that low-grade dread that used to live in your chest? Who are the people around you when your relationships are steady, reciprocal, and genuinely restoring? What stress disappears from your life when you stop tolerating what consistently drains you? What habits support the energy you want to have, rather than depleting what little you managed to hold onto? What opportunities become available to you when you trust your own judgment enough to pursue them?

These aren't just dreams. They're questions that point you forward. Once you see the direction, your daily choices feel less random and more purposeful. The standard that once felt like a loss now feels like protection for something you truly care about.

How the Pieces Work Together

Here's the full picture: everything you've built throughout this book, in the order it works.

Boundaries protect your time and energy when they're threatened. They're the frontline response.

Standards determine what gets close enough to threaten them in the first place. They operate upstream, before the boundary conversation is even needed.

Embodiment happens when these stop being things you practice and become part of who you are. The healed version of you shows up naturally, without needing conscious effort every time.

Vision gives everything direction. It answers the question, "what am I building?" and provides a clear picture that keeps your choices purposeful, not just reactive.

When these work together, something shifts in how you make decisions. You stop asking:

What should I do?

And start asking:

Does this move me toward the life I'm building, or does it pull me away from it?

That one question becomes your compass. It helps you move past guilt, obligation, old habits, and the noise of other people's expectations. You don't need to have everything figured out. You just need to know your direction. After all the work you've done in this book, you know more about that direction than ever before.

Reflection: Design What Comes Next

Take some time with these questions before you finish this chapter. Write down your answers. They're your map.

Ask yourself:

- What did your old self tolerate that you're no longer willing to accept? What does saying no to it make possible?

- Which standard, if you followed it every day, would change your daily life over the next thirty days?

- What does the life you're building look like—not just what you avoid, but what you include?

- Who do you become when you stop trying to fit into places that were never meant for you?

- What do you want your life to feel like—not just how it looks to others, but how it feels to you on a regular day when nothing big is happening?

Your answers aren't just for reflection. They give you direction. Use them.

Take This With You

- **The difference between a boundary and a standard is the difference between reacting to your life and designing it on purpose.**

- Standards work ahead of time. They save you from having the same boundary conversation again and again by deciding in advance what belongs in your life.

- Standards become anchors. They don't break under pressure, chase approval, or ask for understanding. They stand firm.

- **When someone leaves because you stopped abandoning yourself, they weren't there for you. They were there for your willingness to comply.**

- Boundaries without vision turn into walls. With vision, they become the framework for something you're building on purpose.

- When boundaries, standards, embodiment, and vision work together, decision-making becomes clearer, simpler, and more unmistakably yours.

- ***Remember this:*** **Does this move me toward the life I'm building, or does it pull me away? That question is your compass now. Use it.**

You've done the work. You learned how to name what was costing you. You built the language to protect what matters. You held your ground when it shook. You repaired it when it slipped. You moved through the identity vacuum of becoming someone different, and you came out the other side with a clearer picture of who you genuinely are.

Now you get to build from that place. Not from fear. Not from proving anything. Not from the exhausted version of yourself who kept everything running at her own expense.

From self-respect. From standards. From a vision of a life that's entirely yours.

You don't chase worthiness anymore. You move from it.

And everything you build from here finally has room to last.

Conclusion

Every "no" you choose today is a "yes" to the person you're becoming.

Most people pick up a boundaries book hoping for the perfect script. A magic sentence that suddenly makes everyone respect their limits and stop pushing past their comfort zone. They want the one line that fixes everything overnight.

And listen, if I had that sentence, I'd give it to you wrapped in glitter and then head off to a private island like a boundary-setting fairy godmother.

But magic words aren't what change your life. You are.

You didn't just learn boundaries. You rebuilt your foundation of self-respect. You strengthened your voice in situations that used to leave you silent. You held limits even when guilt was loud and old habits lobbied hard for the familiar. You practiced repair instead of shame. And somewhere along the way, not in one dramatic moment but through many ordinary choices, you became someone different.

That is brave work. Uncomfortable work. Deeply human work.

And yes, guilt still whispered sometimes. Anxiety still tried to predict disaster. Old habits still tugged at you, saying, *Hey... remember us?* But you kept going. Because you understand something now that you didn't when you opened to page one: **guilt isn't proof you went too far. It's proof you went somewhere new.**

New can feel strange. New can feel risky. New can feel like too much. Do it anyway.

These aren't small changes. They're generational shifts. When you break patterns rooted in silence, people-pleasing, and self-erasure, you don't just change your own life. You change what's possible for everyone around you. You show a new way of being, where self-respect is normal, rest is allowed, and limits are expected instead of negotiated.

Before you step back into your world, do one thing today. Not tomorrow. Not when things calm down. Today.

Pick one honest act of self-respect:

Let the call go to voicemail and enjoy the silence.

Say "I can't take that on" without the explanation that usually follows.

Close your laptop at the end of the workday and don't reopen it.

Put your phone on Do Not Disturb and feel what it's like to not be available for an hour.

That moment, that single, deliberate choice, is how your new life continues. Not with a dramatic overhaul. Not with a perfect plan. With one clear decision at a time, repeated until it feels like you.

And when you wobble, because you will, come back here. Revisit the words that steadied you. Flip back to the scripts. Remind yourself what you already know about your worth. Growth isn't about getting it right every time. It's about returning to yourself faster each time you drift.

This book isn't something you read once and set aside on a shelf. It's a reset button. A reminder. A quiet voice that says: you're allowed to take care of yourself without feeling guilty as hell about it.

You don't owe anyone burnout. You don't owe anyone unlimited access. What you owe yourself, and only yourself, is your peace, your energy, your honesty, your rest, and your self-respect.

So here's my final wish for you:

May your "no" feel like a full-body exhale. May your "yes" come from desire, not fear. May your boundaries reflect your worth, not your worry. May you meet yourself with grace instead of criticism. May you trust the woman you're becoming, the one who no longer shrinks to keep the peace.

You are worthy of protection. You are worthy of rest. You are worthy of a life that doesn't drain the hell out of you.

Go set one brave boundary today. Your future self is already thanking you.

You didn't pick this book to stay the same.

And you won't.

Epilogue
The Soft Life Reclaimed

Softness isn't a luxury. It's who you become when you no longer live in survival mode.

At some point, most women learned that softness is weakness, rest is indulgent, and taking it easy means you're not working hard enough. We were told that staying busy made us valuable, that exhaustion showed loyalty, and that you don't stop until everything is finished. But everything is never finished. So we kept going. We kept showing up. We kept holding things together, even when we were quietly falling apart, because that's what responsible people do.

But here's what no one explained clearly enough, and what this book has been leading up to:

Softness wasn't discouraged because it was fragile. It was discouraged because people who are exhausted are easier to control.

When you're always tired, you don't question expectations. You don't push back against what's unfair. You don't pause to ask if any of this was really your job. You just keep moving, because stopping feels risky and staying busy has always seemed safer. Over time, that constant motion stops feeling like a choice and becomes part of your personality. You become the reliable one, the dependable one, the person who can handle anything. And you do handle it all, until one day you realize you're managing everything but hardly enjoying any of it.

That's where softness starts. It doesn't begin with a big announcement or a dramatic exit, but with a quiet decision:

I'm done running myself into the ground just to prove I'm worthy.

What Softness Looks Like in Everyday Life

Living softly isn't glamorous. There's no soundtrack. No one gives you awards for letting texts wait until you're ready to reply, for canceling plans when you need rest, for eating dinner slowly without juggling other tasks, or for walking away from an argument because you knew your peace mattered more than winning.

None of these choices are dramatic. They don't look like healing from the outside. But each one sends a message to the part of you that was told for years it wasn't safe to slow down:

You are safe now. You can stop. Your needs matter now.

Repeating that message in everyday moments, even when no one else notices, is what really changes your relationship with yourself. It's not about big boundary talks or dramatic exits. It's about going to bed when your body tells you to, instead of staying up to finish something for someone who isn't even thinking about you. It's about sitting with your coffee on Saturday morning before checking your phone. It's about realizing you no longer dread Sunday evenings because your week now mostly belongs to you.

That's what maintenance looks like. And maintenance is how you keep yourself from burning the hell out.

Take This With You

- Softness doesn't come before boundaries. It appears after you consistently start protecting your peace.

- **You're not abandoning people. You're abandoning burnout.**

- *My needs are not optional anymore.* Say it until it feels true for you.

- Peace will stop feeling boring and start to feel familiar. Just give it time.

- **A soft life isn't built in dramatic moments. It's built through ordinary,**

quiet choices that no one else notices.

This isn't the end of the work. It's the moment the work becomes livable, when boundaries stop feeling like rules you have to enforce and start feeling like part of who you are. When peace isn't something you have to recover, but something you protect. When you stop asking how to survive and start building a life that actually fits you.

The woman who started this book isn't the same as the woman finishing it. You've done something most people never do: you looked honestly at what was costing you, learned what to do about it, and stayed with the discomfort long enough for real change to happen.

That matters. You matter. And the life you're building—quieter, steadier, and more truly yours—is worth every uncomfortable conversation, every shaky boundary, and every moment you chose yourself, even when everything you'd learned told you not to.

Go live it.

A Note on Reviews

If this book helped you say no when you used to say yes, set a limit that once felt impossible, or simply reminded you that your needs matter, someone else needs to hear that too.

She's still where you once were. Still over-explaining. Still second-guessing herself. Still wondering if she's "too much" for simply wanting to be treated with basic respect. She will look for a book just like this one, and your words could be what encourage her to pick it up.

Leaving a review takes about a minute. Find the book on Amazon or wherever you bought it, choose a star rating, and write one or two honest sentences about what stood out to you. It doesn't have to be long or perfect—just share what changed for you.

Your voice has always been at the heart of this book. Use it once more.

Thank you for doing the work and for helping this book reach those who need it most.

Further Reading

Alford, Annalise. "The Invisible Work of Being a Daughter." American Psychological Association, 2024.

American Counseling Association. "The Sensitivity of Boundary Setting in Collectivist Cultures." Counseling Today.

Amodeo, John. "The Surprising Power of Pausing Before Speaking." Psychology Today, 2019.

Aron, Elaine N. "Graceful Boundaries." Psychology Today, 2019.

Bacon, Ian, and Julia Conway. "Co-Dependency and Enmeshment: A Fusion of Concepts." International Journal of Mental Health and Addiction, 2022.

Barrocas, Gabrielle. "The Psychological Impact of Sacrifice in Romantic Relationships." Intersect: The Stanford Journal of Science, 2024.

Bernstein, Gabby. "Stop Ghosting Your Feelings: 60-Second Reset for When You're Spiraling." Dear Media, 2026.

Birnbaum, Gurit E. "The Fragile Spell of Desire: Changes in Sexual Desire Across Relationship Development." Personality and Social Psychology Review, 2018.

Burn, Shawn M. "What to Do When Someone Pushes Your Boundaries." Psychology Today, 2022.

Clayton, Ingrid. "What Is the Fawning Trauma Response?" Psychology Today, 2023.

Cohen, Ilene S. "When Guilt Keeps You From Setting Boundaries." Psychology Today, 2017.

Crane, Martin F., et al. "Reflection to Resilience: Non-Ruminative Self-Reflection and Resilience in Emerging Adults." Journal of Social and Clinical Psychology, 2026.

Drescher, Alex. "Boundaries vs. Control in Relationships." Simply Psychology, 2024.

Foley, Maureen. "Demystifying the Fawn Response." Psychology Today, 2025.

Foley, Maureen. "3 Boundaries You Must Set With a Manipulator." Psychology Today, 2025.

Foley, Maureen. "Setting Boundaries in Your Romantic Relationship." Psychology Today, 2026.

Foti, Stefanie. "Why Setting Boundaries Feels So Uncomfortable." BHealthCounsel, 2026.

Frye, David. "Understanding the Trauma Brain." Psychology Today, 2021.

Geist, Alicia, et al. "Personal Boundaries: The Impact of the Number of and Adherence to Boundaries on Success Outcomes." Psychology Research Think Tank, 2024.

Gerlach, Jennifer. "What If the Person You Need to Set Boundaries With Is Yourself?" Psychology Today, 2024.

Gionta, Dana. "Five Essential Boundaries in the Workplace." Psychology Today, 2023.

Greater Good Science Center. "How to Set Boundaries When You've Never Been Taught How." University of California, Berkeley. greatergood.berkeley.edu.

Guttman, Jonathan. "Setting Boundaries Raises the Bar of Your Comfort Zones." Psychology Today, 2022.

Guttman, Jonathan. "Why Setting Boundaries Triggers Guilt and Anxiety." Psychology Today, 2026.

Hammond, Jeffrey, and W. J. Brown. "Building an Operational Definition of Grounding." Traumatology, 2025.

Hampton, Keith, et al. "Psychological Stress and Social Media Use." Pew Research Center, 2015.

Henry, James P. "Biological Basis of the Stress Response." Integrative Physiological and Behavioral Science, 1992.

Hochschild, Arlie Russell, and Anne Machung. The Second Shift: Working Families and the Revolution at Home. Penguin Books, 2012.

Huckabee, Melanie. "The Trouble With Toxic Boundary Setting." Psychology Today, 2025.

Hülsheger, Ute R., and Anna F. Schewe. "On the Costs and Benefits of Emotional Labor: A Meta-Analysis of Three Decades of Research." Journal of Occupational Health Psychology, 2011.

Johnson, Katie J. "Good Friends Have Boundaries: Provider Strategies for Creating Support Boundaries in Friendships." Communication Studies, 2024.

Johnson, Susan. "Name It to Tame It: The Emotions Underlying Your Triggers." Psychology Today, 2025.

Katz, Laura. "When Boundaries Backfire." Psychology Today, 2021.

Kellenbach, Katharina von, and Matthias Buschmeier. Guilt: A Force of Cultural Transformation. Oxford University Press, 2022.

King, Karen. "Understanding Our Internal Boundaries." Psychology Today, 2022.

Kolk, Bessel van der. The Body Keeps the Score: Brain, Mind, and Body in the Healing of Trauma. Penguin Books, 2014.

Lancaster, Victoria. "Improve Conflict by Setting Boundaries." Psychology Today, 2021.

Lee, Angela, Elif Yildiz, and Anum U. Chaudhary. "Strategies of Boundary Setting in Women Healing from Familial Emotional Abuse." Psychology of Woman Journal, 2023.

Lee, David S., et al. "I-Through-We: How Supportive Social Relationships Facilitate Personal Growth." Personality and Social Psychology Bulletin, 2018.

Lobel, Deborah S. "The Interpersonal Superpower of Validation." Psychology Today, 2024.

Lumanlan, Janet. "How to Deal With Pushback Against Your Boundaries During the Holidays." Psychology Today, 2025.

Ma, Linda. "2 Ways to Shield a Relationship from the Silent Treatment." Psychology Today, 2025.

Ma, Linda. "3 Ways to Get Over the Habit of Over-Explaining." Psychology Today, 2026.

Marcos, Maria J., Tania Zittoun, and Alex Gillespie. "Diaries as Technologies for Sense-Making and Self-Transformation in Times of Vulnerability." Integrative Psychological and Behavioral Science, 2024.

Marone, Lara. "The Real Purpose of Boundaries." Psychology Today, 2026.

Martin, Sharon. "6 Ways to Set Boundaries Without Guilt." Psychology Today, 2022.

Martin, Sharon. "Why Setting Family Boundaries Triggers You, and What Helps." Psychology Today, 2025.

Martin, Sharon. "Enmeshed Families: When Control Is Disguised as Closeness." Psychology Today, 2025.

Mathe, J. R., and W. E. Kelly. "Mental Boundaries: Relationship with Self-Esteem and Social Support." Journal of Social and Personal Relationships, 2023.

Mayo Clinic Staff. "Being Assertive: Reduce Stress, Communicate Better." Mayo Clinic, 2024.

Mellner, Christin, et al. "Predicting Work-Life Conflict: Work-Nonwork Boundary Congruence and Perceived Boundary Control." Frontiers in Psychology, 2021.

Messina, James J. "The People-Pleasing Behavioral Personality Characteristics." MyPA Counseling.

Neale, Paula. "The Hidden Emotional Labor Draining Women Leaders." Psychology Today, 2026.

Nikolić, Maja, et al. "Parental Socialization of Guilt and Shame in Early Childhood." Scientific Reports, 2023.

O'Connell, Megan. "Boundaries and Knowing What You Need to Show Up." Psychology Today, 2026.

Oswald, Rachel. "Setting Boundaries for Well-Being." Mayo Clinic Health System, 2021.

Peel, Rachel, and Nerina Caltabiano. "The Relationship Sabotage Scale." BMC Psychology, 2021.

Perina, Kaja. "A Guide to Healthy Boundaries." Psychology Today, 2025.

Pezirkianidis, Christos, et al. "Adult Friendship and Wellbeing: A Systematic Review with Practical Implications." Frontiers in Psychology, 2023.

Price, Rebecca B., and Ronald Duman. "Neuroplasticity in Cognitive and Psychological Mechanisms of Depression." Molecular Psychiatry, 2020.

Rapp, David J., John M. Hughey, and Glen E. Kreiner. "Boundary Work as a Buffer Against Burnout: Evidence from Healthcare Workers During the COVID-19 Pandemic." Journal of Applied Psychology, 2021.

Ratson, Moshe. "The Ultimate Formula for Conflict Resolution." Psychology Today, 2025.

Raypole, Crystal. "Fight, Flight, Freeze, or Fawn? Understanding Trauma Responses." Healthline, 2021.

Rebaldo, Victoria. "Learning Boundaries to Break the Cycle of Family Dysfunction." Psychology Today, 2026.

Robertson, Donald. "Setting Boundaries: Self-Care or Selfish?" Psychology Today, 2022.

Sanderson, Catherine A. "Setting Boundaries Doesn't Mean What You Think." Association for Psychological Science, 2025.

Saraiya, Tanya C., et al. "Are We Gatekeeping Trauma? A Conceptual Model to Expand Criterion A for Invisible, Identity-Based, and Systemic Traumas." Social Science & Medicine, 2025.

Schumann, Karina. "The Psychology of Offering an Apology." Current Directions in Psychological Science, 2018.

Sills, Diane. "The Role Healthy Friction Plays in a Relationship." Psychology Today, 2022.

Smith, Michael A. "Caregiver Burnout in the Age of Self-Help." Psychology Today, 2026.

Speight, Suzette L. "An Exploration of Boundaries and Solidarity in Counseling Relationships." Journal of Counseling & Development, 2012.

Stojanovic, Milica, and Wendy Wood. "Beyond Deliberate Self-Control: Habits Automatically Achieve Long-Term Goals." Current Opinion in Psychology, 2024.

Streep, Peg. "Resentful Love: The Burden of Adult Children of Neglect." Psychology Today, 2024.

Sullivan, Luke, and Fay Niker. "Friendships Need to Go Wrong in Order to Go Right." Journal of the American Philosophical Association, 2025.

Swales, Stephanie A. "Unraveling the Complexity of Boundary Maintenance." Psychology Today, 2024.

Thapar-Olmos, Nisha. "Why "Healthy Boundaries" Look Different Across Cultures." Psychology Today, 2025.

Travers, Mark. "How to Tell the Difference Between a Rule and a Boundary." Psychology Today, 2025.

Travers, Mark. "3 Ways People Pleasers Can Ignore Boundary Backlash." Forbes, 2025.

Travers, Mark. "3 Ways Remote Work Exposes People-Pleasing Habits." Psychology Today, 2026.

Vandepitte, Sara, et al. "The Role of Peace of Mind and Meaningfulness in Explaining Subjective Well-Being." Journal of Happiness Studies, 2022.

Walsh, Lara C., et al. "Does Putting Down Your Smartphone Make You Happier? The Effects of Restricting Digital Media on Well-Being." PLOS ONE, 2024.

Wharton, Amy S. "The Sociology of Emotional Labor." Annual Review of Sociology, 2009.

Wilson, Brooke. "Discomfort: A Pathway to Growth." Psychology Today, 2023.

Woods, Tyler. "Your Brain on Conflict." Psychology Today, 2025.

Woolley, Kaitlin, and Ayelet Fishbach. "Motivating Personal Growth by Seeking Discomfort." Psychological Science, 2022.

Yin, Henry H., and Barbara J. Knowlton. "The Role of the Basal Ganglia in Habit Formation." Nature Reviews Neuroscience, 2006.

Yperen, Nico W. van, and Mariët Hagedoorn. "Living Up to High Standards and Psychological Distress." Personality and Social Psychology Bulletin, 2008.

Zheng, Lei, Qian Lu, and Yu Gan. "Effects of Expressive Writing and Use of Cognitive Words on Meaning Making and Post-Traumatic Growth." Psychological Research, 2019.

About the Author

M. Luna Zidane writes self-help for people healing from narcissistic abuse, emotional manipulation, and long-term self-erasure — the kind of healing that doesn't happen through positivity or perfection, but through clarity, consistency, and self-respect that holds up in real life.

Drawing on lived experience, psychological research, and pattern-based insight, her work helps readers stop people-pleasing, release guilt conditioning, and build internal standards that actually protect their peace—not just in theory, but on a difficult Tuesday when the pressure to cave is louder than everything else.

She believes healing isn't about becoming harder or colder. It's about becoming clearer — anchored, grounded, and no longer available for dynamics that require self-erasure to survive.

Her work is direct, practical, and built for people who are done shrinking — and finally ready to stop.

Where This Work Continues

T he book ends here. The work doesn't.

If you need reminders on tough days, real talk about setting boundaries, and practical tools for when things get stressful, connect with M. Luna Zidane where she regularly shares her insights:

TikTok: @theglowstandard

Instagram: @_theglowstandard_

No need to perform. No pressure to be perfect. Just honest conversations about choosing yourself, time after time, in the everyday moments that truly matter.

Show up when you need it. Move at your own pace.